DEAR TOMMY

AGNES DOCHERTY WITH TOM DOCHERTY

DEAR TOMMY

AGNES DOCHERTY WAS MARRIED TO BRITAIN'S MOST CONTROVERSIAL FOOTBALL MANAGER. THIS IS THE PORTRAIT OF THEIR MARRIAGE THAT SHE WANTED TO BE PUBLISHED AFTER SHE DIED.

JOHN BLAKE

Published by John Blake Publishing Ltd,
3 Bramber Court, 2 Bramber Road,
London W14 9PB, England

www.johnblakepublishing.co.uk

First published in hardback in 2008
Published in paperback in 2009

ISBN: 978-1-84454-713-5

British Library Cataloguing-in-Publication Data:

A catalogue record for this book is available from the British Library.

Design by www.envydesign.co.uk

Printed in Great Britain by CPI Bookmarque, Croydon CR0 4TD

1 3 5 7 9 10 8 6 4 2

Papers used by John Blake Publishing are natural, recyclable
products made from wood grown in sustainable forests.
The manufacturing processes conform to the environmental
regulations of the country of origin.

Plate section two, page one © mirrorpix; page 4, below and
page 7, below © PA Photos

Every attempt has been made to contact the relevant copyright-holders,
but some were unobtainable. We would be grateful if the appropriate
people could contact us.

'My grateful thanks for everything you have been to me. My family has been the centre of my life, each and every one of you. Do not be sad – I was greatly blessed in my lifetime by all of you. Enjoy your lives and love each other.'

Extract from a letter attached to the last will and testament of Agnes Docherty.

* * *

To both my mum, Agnes, and my wife, Rachel, for their unwavering love and support. I've also been greatly blessed.

Tom Docherty

CONTENTS

FOREWORD

Agnes Docherty was my mother.

When I was a little boy in the harsh winter of 1961, she never told me that my immediate future was built on footballing quicksand. She didn't need to. Somehow I just sensed it. I sensed we might be moving house, that I could be changing schools and losing new-found friends on the whim of a clattering teleprinter at about 4.40 on any given Saturday afternoon.

As fickle as the watching fans, it would stumble across the screen, sometimes stopping, whether by accident or design I'll never know, at the most crucial moment. Back then, the fact that *Grandstand* was in black and white only added to the drama. It was like watching a ransom demand being typed live to the nation and I loved it from the first moment I saw it.

But not nearly as much as I loved my mum.

One of the hardest tasks that I had to confront after her sudden death from a heart attack in September 2002 was having to remove her name from various documents. Forced to face the fact that she had gone. Forever and a day.

I haven't managed to do it with everything. For example, her name, address and phone number still reside on the inside back page of my passport as one of the two people – along with my wife, Rachel – to contact in case of accident and there those details will remain until that document also expires.

Somehow I succeeded with my mobile phone but it took me the worst part of a day to do it. Countless times and several lost weeks after her death, I found myself taking the deepest breath, scrolling alphabetically past my brother Michael's numbers to the name 'Mum', pressing options and being offered the opportunity to erase the number. Even then, when I had finally summoned up the courage to press 'select' followed by 'erase', the phone had one cruel trick left to play. Only her number had been deleted so I was reduced to staring at a small screen asking me if I wanted to erase *all* details. That is to say, did I wish to erase 'Mum'? I knew I had to, that it was a number I would sadly never need to call again. So, having eventually pressed 'OK', I watched as the animation deposited her name into a tiny dustbin. And then I cried almost enough tears to fill a real one.

Tommy Docherty was my father.

He's still alive and yet I think of him in the past tense. But mostly not at all. With my dad, when I was that same little boy, it was different. I felt more of an innate sense of loyalty than unconditional love.

As a nomadic child whose life was dictated by results, I was destined never to have many close friends and perhaps that's just as well because those I do have today will undoubtedly read this and accuse me of being nothing more than a footballing fraudster. Offered the unlikely opportunity, I will always dispute the charge and yet, emerging from my sporting closet after all these years and considering the self-inflicted evidence, I concede they may unfortunately have a point.

You see, I supported Chelsea for years – well, over six actually – then Rotherham United for 11 months, followed by Queens Park Rangers for a full 28 days, Aston Villa for just over a year, FC Porto for a season and a half, Hull City half-heartedly for roughly ten weeks, Scotland whenever an international happened to come around and finally Manchester United for what will be the rest of my life.

My handful of mates have stayed loyal to their roots. Follow your hometown club, they say. You were born there and grew up there. That's fine. I can understand that – except that I was born in Preston and grew up pretty much everywhere. My loyalty was to my dad and so I would instantly switch allegiance as he moved inexorably from club to club.

Only now, writing this all these years later, does it occur to me that we never had the chance to get to know one another. A fleeting presence at best, his job consumed him to the exclusion of any affection or 'quality time' as it's called today.

There wasn't a daily diet of football in those days so he *must* have been around some of the time. I just don't remember it. In fact, I saw more of him in the newspapers than I ever did at home. If my siblings or I were misbehaving, my mum's warning of 'Wait till your father gets home!' never had quite the desired effect.

It's over 30 years now since I last spoke to him, over 30 years since that summer of 1977 when he left my mum for another woman. It was the beginning of the end of his career and, to me, whenever he inevitably pops up as a rent-a-quote on a football programme, he still appears bitter and slightly bewildered by the ramifications of that decision.

So many people down the years have urged me to forgive him but I firmly believe he has never forgiven himself. Although I witnessed my mum's heartache, I feel ashamed at never having fully appreciated the depth of her torture and suffering until I read her notes that form the essence of this book. It was as deep as her love for the man who ruined her life long before she died.

I found those random yet detailed handwritten notes in a battered old folder in the loft as we tearfully emptied her house. I believe my mum wrote them in the hope that the exercise would prove to be cathartic. I have my doubts that it worked – some wounds never heal – but transcribing her memoirs certainly helped me as I struggled to come to terms with her death.

Writing, or interpreting, this book in conjunction with my late mother has been an unusual collaboration. At times a delight, at others distressing. But, from reading her first words, it imbued me with a sense of destiny.

It's quite a story – but then she was quite a lady…

Tom Docherty
March 2009

PREFACE

Football supporters aren't normal.

I can't define exactly what it is, there's just something missing in their lives. Trust me, I know. Through personal involvement, I counted myself as one of their number for so many years but I've managed to move on. I've had to. The fans on the other hand will always be here because, as I say, they're not all there.

In the space of roughly 90 minutes and irrespective of overhead conditions, the game can warm your heart or chill you to the bone. Because, like the weather, it also has inevitable highs and lows.

Wherever we happened to live, and as you will discover with Tommy's turbulent career that would be in a considerable amount of places, I always had a calendar hanging on either side of the kettle in our latest kitchen. The one on the left was for the current month and the other was for the next year, simply because the football season began in August and ended the following May. That much at least has never changed in the sport that was to consume such a large part of my life.

So, for almost 30 years as the start of a new campaign excitedly approached and the fixture list was announced, I would sit down and meticulously fill in dates on those twin calendars for the next 10 months with the appropriate matches for whichever club my husband was playing for, coaching or eventually managing. Celtic v ... Preston North End v ... Arsenal v ... Chelsea v ... Rotherham United v ... Queens Park Rangers v ... Aston Villa v ... FC Porto v ... Hull City v ... Scotland v ... and finally Manchester United v ...

I never dreamed the day would arrive when I would find myself staring in tearful disbelief at the entry circled in bright red on the right: Docherty v Docherty. A contest to be played behind closed doors in front of three magistrates at a neutral venue. A match that I thought had been made in heaven was now a court case because, certainly not for the first time in our marriage, it wasn't his *team* that had been playing away from home...

CHAPTER 1

HOME AND AWAY

Yet each man kills the thing he loves,
By each let this be heard,
Some do it with a bitter look,
Some with a flattering word
OSCAR WILDE (1854–1900)

Tommy Docherty, my husband of more than 27 years, looked directly at me for the first time in such a long time and blinked nervously before delivering the words that will remain with me for the rest of my days: 'If I don't leave you, she says her mother is going to the press.'

Staring back at this clearly tortured man who had been the centre of my life for the best – and sporadically the worst – part of three decades, I instinctively knew that I would be the one who would have to ask the definitive question. Even then, clearly drowning in the depths of his own deceit, he didn't possess the courage to name the other guilty party until it was forced upon him. And so I heard myself whisper: 'Who is *she*…?'

He hesitated and then slowly, it seemed shamefully, replied, 'Mary Brown. Agnes, I'm sorry...'

Sorry? Sorry to tear my life asunder with five short words? I was stunned – so stunned that it never entered my mind to enquire exactly what on earth it had to do with her *mother* or why indeed she would want to go to the newspapers. Was he suggesting that he was being threatened with blackmail? And that it would make a blind bit of difference to me if he was? As far as I was concerned, he had finally admitted his adultery, and pressure from a third party (or should that be fourth?) didn't grant him some kind of get-out-of-jail-free card.

I had waited for what seemed an eternity for Tommy to explain his increasingly erratic behaviour of recent months, and yet I was also painfully aware that the reason had been staring me in the face. I just hadn't wanted to accept the brutal truth and inevitable outcome. Quite simply, I knew there was another woman. I had seen the symptoms once before.

But Mary Brown? The 31-year-old mother of two and wife of Laurie, the Manchester United physiotherapist, was the last name I could have possibly imagined. I had never really known the Browns that well, merely sharing polite conversation with them at several club functions and Christmas parties.

Tommy's presence and consequently our conversations at home had become so infrequent that it was only from casually listening to the local radio news bulletin earlier that day that I discovered he had received a driving ban. I can't recall the offence, but suffice to say that neither speeding nor alcohol could ever exactly be considered strangers to Tommy's steering wheel, so I calmly enquired who had brought him back. He informed me that Mrs Brown's mother, Mrs Hopkins, was waiting for him in the car park of our local pub, the Bull's Head, about 500 yards further up the road. She seemed to be playing an increasingly influential cameo role in this sordid production.

I had given Tommy an ultimatum on that same Thursday afternoon when he had phoned to say he would be coming home on Saturday night as there was 'something important' he had to tell me. In my most vivid nightmare I couldn't have dreamed, as I would later discover, that he had already sold the story of his affair to the *Sunday People* for £25,000. That, in fact, *he* was the mercenary who had voluntarily gone to the press and was now planning to gently break the front-page story to me before it was published the following morning.

I had seldom, if ever, delivered veiled threats but I was at the end of my tether and sensed that, whatever he had to say, it certainly wasn't going to be good news. His behaviour had bordered on the unforgivable in the past year, so I warned him that if he didn't return that same night I would go searching for him. That could have been embarrassing for either or both of us, but he decided not to call my bluff and arrived on the doorstep that evening. Two and a half days before the *Sunday People*.

He had come to deliver his no doubt frequently rehearsed tale of deception before returning to the small Derbyshire village of Mottram-in-Longdendale, where Mrs Brown was apparently waiting to inform her husband that she was leaving him.

So there Tommy sat, shifting awkwardly on the beige leather footstool in our darkened lounge. I perched nervously on the matching settee opposite and instinctively reached for his hand. Old habits, I suppose. He pulled away, just staring into space, then suddenly sprang to his feet, mumbling, 'I have to go. Really, I have to go...' But I had questions that demanded and deserved answers, so I politely asked him to sit down again. Rather ironic, don't you think, that here was the manager of arguably the most famous football team in the world completely incapable of dealing with this particular ball game.

To continue the analogy, I was being substituted for a younger and, to my 49-year-old husband, more attractive player. Yet the Messiah of the Stretford End was totally incapable of justifying his tactics. A man rarely lost for words in all the years I thought I had known him was now barely able to construct a coherent sentence. How long had it been going on? 'About a year,' he informed the fireplace. Had he been sleeping with her? The manner in which he continued to avoid eye contact and shuffled his unpolished shoes was an admission in itself before he cleared his throat and muttered, 'Yes. I'm sorry.' And where had this been taking place? 'I have a key to her mother's flat,' he told me. Did Laurie know? 'He's known for a long time,' Tommy replied.

My immediate reaction was one of total revulsion, yet I also felt a burning, almost illogically maternal desire to extricate him from this self-inflicted mess, as I had once before in 1967. He looked like a man skirting the outer edge of a nervous breakdown. All he could stammer was: 'I have to go. I have to go...' It was then that I realised without a trace of malice or satisfaction that he wouldn't emerge from this situation unscathed. Not this time. In complete turmoil and with an irrational sense of failure, I asked him what I had done that could have contributed to such an awful state of affairs.

4

'You've done nothing wrong, you're marvellous,' he replied. 'You gave me too much rope and I've hanged myself...'

I told Tommy it wasn't called rope, it was called trust! We were as one, or so I had always innocently believed. I felt unnaturally calm and also pervaded with an inexplicable and overwhelming feeling of relief that at last, after the most awful year I could have ever envisaged, I finally knew exactly what had been troubling my husband. The deception was over. It was out in the open now and therefore I genuinely believed I could deal with it. I had done as much a decade earlier and in remarkably similar circumstances. In spite of everything, I still loved him that much.

Surely, I pleaded, he could not seriously cast aside all our hard work, the wonderful years and friends we had collected along the way. Together, we had earned the kind of memories nobody could possibly buy. I stressed that if he left me he was also deserting his 12-year-old son, Peter (the only one of our four children still living at home) and all our lovely, extended family. He just sat there like a guilty man awaiting his verdict.

I don't believe that I have ever seen a lonelier, unhappier person than my husband in those defining few minutes of our lives. I warned him that he would lose his job, probably the most prestigious one in football. That at least provoked an immediate, if arrogant, response. 'Of course I won't lose my bloody job – we've just won the Cup!'

I said, 'Tommy, trust me. If you leave me, you *will* lose your job!'

I knew he didn't believe me as he spluttered, 'But I've told you, her mother is going to the press!'

There he was, trying to blame somebody else for his predicament. I promised him we could overcome the problem if we stood firm, that somehow we would find the words to ease the situation for him. I moved alongside him and he allowed me to briefly hold his hand before leaping to his feet with the words: 'Look, I love her. I have to go.'

I pleaded with him to discuss it further but he brushed past me and headed for the hallway. I cried out, 'Tommy, *please*!' and attempted to hold him but he pulled away.

'I have to go,' he repeated.

That was when I heard a voice from deep within myself shout, 'OK, go then!', before quickly regaining enough composure to calmly ask him for his door keys.

He stared blankly at me and then breathed a long, soft sigh of resignation and handed over the keys to the beautiful house that we had strived all our lives to be proud to call our home.

My husband quietly went upstairs to see Peter before he walked out of our lives that night. When he finally left, Tommy took my dreams with him. He apologised once more, as if he actually believed that it would make a difference. For so many years we had talked of the times that lay ahead of us when the children had all grown up and left home, of the exciting, exotic places we would visit in our lengthy, well-earned retirement. It would have been wonderful to have shared those twilight years of my life with the Tommy Docherty I once knew and adored. But that had now all gone. Like a thief in the night, he stole my dreams.

As the front door closed behind him I felt completely lost, as though I was floundering in the dark. Abandoned, feeling physically sick and yet strangely incapable of even crying. There was total disbelief in my mind, in my heart, that anyone could callously cast aside so many years together in the course of such a brief conversation. How on earth could he do it?

Thursday, 16 June 1977. For all the wrong reasons, the date is forever engraved in my memory as deeply as the birthdays of our children. My world had shattered and no one was there to help me pick up the countless pieces. And then, just when I thought that it couldn't get any more upsetting, the following afternoon at 5:00 pm I received a phone call from Tommy. He called to tell me that he'd made a terrible mistake. He'd changed his mind and wanted to come home.

CHAPTER 2

AN INVITATION TO THE DANCE

The past is a foreign country:
they do things differently there.
L.P. HARTLEY (1895–1972)

Some instances of my past are like a foreign country to me now. When I look back at them I seem to see the images only in black and white.

One such memory is the evening of 6 November 1948. I can hear 'Twelfth Street Rag' by Pee Wee Hunt and picture myself as a 19-year-old having the time of her life. Except that it's blurred around the edges – as if the lens has somehow been smudged by the passage of time – and the sound is no more than a distant echo. I had a waist in inches that matched my age in years and I'm absolutely certain that it would have been a Saturday night, because I'm dancing.

It wasn't a Saturday night *unless* I was dancing. It was generally the only night of the week that I was allowed to go out and I was under strict instructions to be home by 10:30

pm, even though the dance didn't finish until 11:00 pm. That meant leaving at approximately 10:00 pm, and every single week I resented missing that last hour. Not that I would ever have contemplated disobeying Agnes and Matthew McKeown. But not because my parents ruled by fear. Quite simply, they cared. And they taught their children to care, too.

As the eldest of seven children and eventual mother of a wonderful four of my own, I came to know that the moment just before those final all-important 60 minutes of the dance was the time when any respectable young lady should have made her excuses and left. I hated having to do it at the time, but I thank my parents for making me do it now. When I think back on those times now, it's always with a wistful air. How attitudes have changed since the innocence and gently enforced discipline of my youth. The thought occurs to me: why does every generation fail to realise *their* parents were once young themselves?

Yet for all my parents' laudable concern, I had no need of their protection. I wasn't drawn to the dance halls by the boys but by the music. Until that evening, at least. A significant portion of my weekly pocket money was spent on admission and soft drinks, but I didn't care about the cost because all of my life I have loved to dance – and never more so than on that particular Saturday night so many years ago.

I recall that it was my friend, Laura McGread, who introduced me to my future husband. His name was Thomas Henderson Docherty, the vibrant young man who would take me on the rollercoaster ride of a lifetime before coming off the rails so recklessly that he would break my heart and destroy his own career in the process.

So, as I silently sat and listened on the telephone half a lifetime later to my errant husband begging for forgiveness, for an opportunity to make amends only a matter of hours after I had similarly pleaded with *him* to reconsider, I found my mind slowly wandering back to that foreign country. The past. Wandering and then wondering if, with the assistance of hindsight, I would have done things differently there.

And, as strange as it may seem now, I wouldn't have altered a single thing. The boy I met and eventually married was not the man he would become before our journey finally ended. I had always been perfectly happy to work as hard as necessary, as a devoted wife, loving mother and live-in personal secretary, to provide Tommy with that length of rope he mentioned earlier to scale the peaks of his career. As a footballer, then manager, he had more than succeeded and, in return, I had been blessed with four beautiful, healthy children, the house of my dreams with a heated swimming pool in the back garden, a brand-new white BMW, frequent foreign holidays and enough money never to have to worry about the postman and his brown envelopes again.

How could I have possibly predicted in that frugal past that such an idyllic future would be so cruelly snatched away by this desperate voice on the other end of the line? As he implored me to give him one last chance so my mind remained resolutely stuck in the post-war austerity of my adolescence. Because, at that precise and appalling moment in my life, I could only be certain of one fact: all I had to look forward to was the past.

The Glasgow Celtic squad had arrived in Girvan on the west

coast of Scotland that freezing and fateful morning in early November 1948 for an extended weekend training session. They were staying on the coast at the Shelbourne Hotel. It has been converted into a row of houses now but back then it was a grand old Victorian building that stared serenely out to the Ailsa Craig and was owned by Laura's father.

Even in those monochrome days of my youth, the presence of one of the most famous football teams in the world in our small South Ayrshire town had been the cause of great excitement. This only increased when, at nearly 8:45 pm, at our own little local dance, in our own little local hall, some of those same Celtic players came strolling casually through the door. Laura excitedly claimed to recognise several of them from their portraits on cigarette cards that tobacco companies used to include in their packets. I didn't smoke.

It was the only dance hall in the entire town, so we shouldn't have been too surprised when they walked in. How do I remember the time so accurately? Well, the record playing at that exact moment was one of my all-time favourites, 'About A Quarter To Nine' by Al Jolson, and their entrance could almost have been choreographed. Fate? I'll let you decide, but I also vividly recall wearing a Viyella dress for the first time that night. It was the colour of emeralds or, as many people in Scotland still refer to it, 'Celtic green'.

Having been introduced by Laura, who can only have 'known' him for approximately two minutes herself, Tommy and I talked and danced for just over an hour before it was time for me to make my usual early departure. He asked if he could walk me home and I accepted. It was not something that

I would normally have done because, in those days, even the generally unlit streets of our town were considered safe. Besides, I usually returned home with another friend, Mary Rennie, who lived on the same street.

But there was an uncertain something about Tommy that was different. He was such good company that it even made amends for his frequent clumsiness on the dance floor. At that time, I knew next to nothing about football but assumed he must be better in the tackle than he was at dancing. And, when I could understand his staccato Glaswegian delivery, he was by some distance the funniest person I had ever met. It may have been my considerably softer Ayrshire accent but, for some reason, he thought I was a schoolteacher. We seemed to develop an immediate rapport. It wasn't a case of an impressionable, star-struck teenage girl meeting a famous, wealthy footballer in some trendy city-centre disco. In that harsh winter of 1948, it was an innocent young accounts clerk attempting to delicately avoid the clodhopping feet of a fiercely ambitious Celtic reserve-team player at a local dance at Girvan Catholic Hall.

Tommy had to first receive the permission of his manager, Jimmy Hogan, and then discovered he had the best part of two miles to walk me back to where I lived, at 27 Piedmont Road. Well, he had offered! My parents always waited up for me and, of course, having failed to recognise Mary as my companion from behind the twitching net curtains, naturally wanted to know the identity of the stranger they had seen scampering back into the night. I said, 'His name is Tommy Docherty.' And, being acutely aware of my dad's undying devotion to a certain

Scottish team who have always worn green and white hoops, casually added, 'He's a footballer – and he plays for Celtic.'

Tommy had been at the club for less than four months after serving his two years' National Service in Palestine and had been consigned mainly to the reserves since his return. His handful of opportunities in the first team until then had come when the first-choice right-half, Bobby Evans, had been called away on international duty for Scotland. However, Dad was sufficiently knowledgeable to remark, 'Not a bad player, that one.'

I was shocked to find a small smile of satisfaction flickering across my face. It was far too early to be proud. I only discovered much later that, unable to afford the luxury of a watch, Tommy had sprinted back to the dance hall in order to make the Celtic players' curfew with seconds to spare.

It was Laura's 21st birthday party at her father's hotel the following evening. I was so excited because, not only did that mean dancing two nights in succession, but I also knew the Celtic team, and therefore Tommy in particular, were still staying there. *And* I had permission to stay out until 12:30 am and be home by 1:00 am. I may have only been five feet tall but I felt so grown up!

Inevitably, from the moment I walked in deliberately late, pretending that I was looking for anybody but my future husband, Tommy and I spent most of the evening in one another's company. Although I hadn't been mistaken regarding his lack of prowess in the dancing stakes, I had been equally correct about his charisma. At about seven inches taller then me, he was still a little short – but he was also little short of magnetic.

For a girl from Girvan, where a shopping trip on the bus to

nearby Ayr was considered an annual adventure, the party was beyond anything I had previously experienced. There was even an orchestra specially brought in from Glasgow for the occasion. Yet, in spite of my extended 'leave', once again I had to be off while the band played on. It already seemed so natural that Tommy should walk me home that I'm not even sure he asked me this time.

We took a more leisurely route back along the suitably moonlit beach and only stopped talking when my front door caught us completely by surprise. It seemed polite to invite him in to briefly meet my mum and dad (after all, God bless them, they were just the other side of the curtains again!) and, before he left and with his own deadline clearly in mind, I noticed Tommy glancing nervously at the clock in the hall several times while firstly exchanging pleasantries with my parents and then addresses with me.

Although it didn't matter to me in the slightest and he never seemed overtly ashamed of his origins either, I was to discover that Tommy's address was not, in the timeless jargon of estate agents everywhere, among the most 'sought after' in Glasgow. Quite the opposite. Tommy was from the Gorbals, a name synonymous with violence and deprivation.

Tommy's part of the Gorbals was Shettleston. If you've never heard of that part of such an unforgiving city, simply imagine the most dangerous, inhospitable place you've ever been to and then discard it by way of comparison. For this was the east end of Glasgow, where razor gangs roamed the mean streets and mindlessly robbed neighbours who were no better off than themselves. It was into that cul-de-sac of dreams that Tommy had been born on 24 April 1928. But he was one of the lucky ones. Although there had been no evidence of sporting prowess in his family history, Tommy would prove to be both legally and ferociously capable of robbing a football from the feet of the most gifted forwards of his generation. It was a talent which would be his passport out of that godforsaken Glasgow ghetto.

In the Gorbals, faded hope pervaded the atmosphere and you merely had to breathe in to smell the despair, to sense the unspoken acceptance that life had dealt those people a worthless hand. Tommy was one of the fortunate few. He was able to tackle fate and come away with the ball.

We wrote to one another every day the week after we met. I remember his first letter so well, as I spent two hours trying to decipher it. It was easy to see from his almost illegible scrawl that Tommy had received the most basic of educations. In fact, I considered it to his credit that he could read and write at all. It endeared him to me all the more.

Tommy promised he would be returning to Girvan after his match that Saturday afternoon. I met him from the bus station at 8:45 pm – little wonder that 'About A Quarter To Nine' would forever remain one of our favourite songs – and we headed hurriedly to the local dance. Or at least I did, with a slightly less-than-enthusiastic Tommy in tow. Even in those early days he must have meant quite a lot to me if I was prepared to sacrifice more than half of the evening on my precious dance floor to him! He walked me home again before returning to stay overnight at the Shelbourne and, after meeting at Mass the next morning, we spent the rest of a delightful day at my house in the relaxed company of my parents, four brothers, John, Matt, Tommy and James, and two sisters, Mary and Margaret.

We talked, tucked into my mother's unrivalled homemade food, played board games and laughed. Most of all, for so many years, Tommy and I laughed. As arranged, I was waiting for him outside the hotel at 6:45 am on Monday morning – it's hardly surprising nobody ever wrote a romantic song about *that* hour of the day – and we walked dejectedly back to the bus stop for his return journey to Glasgow. I was missing him before the driver had started the engine.

Fortunately for my boyfriend, for that was what he had rapidly become, Laura informed me that her father's unashamed allegiance to all things even remotely connected to Celtic extended to their players receiving an undisclosed special rate at the Shelbourne. But, in addition to his return bus fare, it had still obviously been an expensive weekend for Tommy. I don't know what he earned, but to supplement his salary during the week he had started a part-time afternoon job at a gents' outfitters on Sauchiehall Street in the city centre after training with Celtic each morning. It was just as well, for we had unwittingly established a pattern of delightful repetition that would last for the next six weeks before I began to fear that, even without him once referring to the cost, he couldn't afford for it to continue indefinitely.

It was an unwritten rule for Tommy that, like me as the eldest child, he would have to leave school when he reached the age of 14 in order to earn a living. If any children were going to benefit from an extended education then, it would be your siblings. In those days, further education was considered quite literally a poor second to extra income, however meagre those additional wages might have been. So it was that I left St Joseph's Convent and started my pre-Tommy working life in early 1943, behind the till at Templeton, the grocers in the town centre.

Roughly six months later, I came home to be told by my brothers that Father O'Connell was in the back room with our parents and they had heard them discussing me. I was immediately worried and thought, 'What have I done wrong?', only to discover from our parish priest that the manager of the local branch of the Royal Bank of Scotland had asked him to recommend a clerk and he had called round to see if I would be interested in the post.

It was clearly understood that the position was temporary until the young men hopefully returned from serving in World War II. In the end I stayed there for three years and enjoyed the job enormously. In early 1946, when a large proportion of our boys did come happily marching home, I joined Galbraith McEwan and Company as an audit clerk, attended evening classes for shorthand and typing and completed various correspondence courses in accountancy.

I was very happy with my career but Tommy's problem up until beginning at the sympathetic tailor's shop had always been finding a position that allowed him to take every Saturday afternoon off to play football. With that immovable obstacle in mind, he had previously acquired literally dozens of jobs on any given Monday in the private but certain knowledge he would have to resign on the following Saturday lunchtime. They wouldn't have understood that not only did he have a game to go to, he was actually playing. Fortunately, the manager of the outfitter's shop was also a big Celtic fan.

Tommy's mother was a very hard-working woman, a school cleaner who also took in washing and scrubbed front steps, almost anything to make ends meet. But she desperately required that additional revenue and so, for all his efforts, Tommy was left with just his pocket money – and now that was all going on buses and a hotel every weekend. I didn't dare broach the subject in any of the three letters that I was writing on a daily basis – although I could probably have done with the extra material to write about. I now wonder exactly what I did manage to mention had happened in the course of the three or four hours since I had last put fountain pen to paper. But, as I trudged back home along Dalrymple Street one rainy evening, deep in troubled thought and reassuring myself that Tommy would tell me – and I would naturally understand – if his visits had to become less frequent, there was my mum to meet me at the door.

Reading my mind and answering my prayers, she smiled and said, 'You know, love, I've been thinking. That boy would be better staying here. It must be very expensive for him at that hotel.' I had not only been named after my mother but, throughout my entire life, I aspired to be half the person she was.

From then on, Tommy began spending his weekends with us, sharing a bedroom with two of my brothers and making early-morning jokes about Matt's snores and John's socks. He complained with a smile that it's physically impossible to hold both your ears and your nose simultaneously. But it was only after later seeing Shettleston on that first unforgettable visit that I realised how enormous a release travelling to see me – in fact, all of us – on the coast must have been for him.

We had two bikes between the seven of us and Tommy and I would sometimes commandeer them and spend Sunday mornings cycling to nearby Byne Hill or some 10 miles to Ballantrae with sandwiches and homemade lemonade for lunch. On other weekends, I would happily sit on the beach and watch him play football while my brothers attempted to join in. They soon learned never to be in possession of the ball for too long as that would have invited a shuddering challenge from my boyfriend.

My mother quickly adored him and treated him almost as another son, sometimes beyond and to the point of blatant favouritism, and yet there wasn't so much as a hint of jealousy from my siblings. For example, she always used to bake Swiss rolls and make delicious doughnuts for Sunday tea, and if Tommy helped himself while they were being sugared then that was just fine by her. But, if any of my brothers so much as began to stretch for one, they would instantly get their knuckles rapped by the back of the spoon!

And, although my dad was a gentle man of few words, everything must have suited him or it simply wouldn't have been the way it was. He was a miner who bred canaries and loved and lived for his family, gardening and Celtic Football Club. And I always instinctively knew it was in that order. He had an allotment in which he grew all manner and size of vegetables and Mum would make enough wonderful broth to easily feed a family of nine – or ten when Tommy was in town.

Dad also dabbled in photography and, as a result, I'm sure

he is responsible for my phobia. I doubt very much if there is a name for a person who suffers from an irrational fear of canaries but, if there is, I'm one of that select group. Many years earlier, when I must have been aged about six, a national newspaper was running a photographic competition and he decided to enter by taking a picture of his wee daughter standing in our garden shed surrounded by several dozen of his free-flying friends. He failed to win the camera equipment on offer but I have been petrified of canaries ever since. I'm not even comfortable in their company if they are in cages, but I never once blamed him. He was my dad and I loved him.

One particular Saturday morning as a birthday surprise, after Tommy and I had been seeing one another for over three months, Dad took me by bus to Glasgow to watch his sporting heroes in action. There were no motorways in those days but, instead of quietly reading or enjoying the scenery, I spent the entire journey vainly trying to elicit the rules of the game from my father. He had wisely decided to bide his time and patiently explain everything to me as the match unfolded in front of us – including the unfathomable offside rule – and I enjoyed every minute of it. My only regrets were that my favourite player was appearing for the reserve team away to Motherwell on the same afternoon and that I didn't feel qualified enough to later analyse Bobby Evans's performance to my desperately inquisitive boyfriend.

Tommy was the eldest of three children. When he first invited me to meet his widowed mother and two sisters, I was completely unprepared for Mrs Docherty and her instant hostility towards me. There had naturally been no warning and, despite Tommy's repeated attempts to inject some humour into the situation, I found the visit increasingly awkward because of her blatant indifference, an attitude I tried to obviate by being as friendly as possible. But that only seemed to antagonise her all the more. When I mentioned this to my own mother, having gratefully returned home, she said maybe Mrs Docherty hadn't meant it personally, that perhaps any girl Tommy took home would have received the same treatment. It may well have been true but it didn't alleviate my anxiety.

His mother had married at just 17 years old and didn't have Tommy until she was 30; Margaret came two years after that and Mary seven years later. She was seven months pregnant with her youngest child when her husband died suddenly. I don't even know the circumstances. In all the time I knew her, Mrs Docherty never once mentioned her husband's name. I never even saw a photograph of him. Perhaps that was her way of dealing with her loss, but I found it strange. I've always believed in cherishing the memory of loved ones – and that naturally includes talking about them and keeping pictures around the house.

Despite her distant animosity, life was blissful and there were never enough hours in the too few days that Tommy and I spent together. We were so much in love. Neither of us was on the telephone, but we had arranged for Tommy to ring me at a local call box twice a week (on Tuesdays and Thursdays, naturally at 8:45 pm) and those letters were still flying back and forth. Then, one warm and memorable evening in the middle of May, on the top deck of a bus travelling from Glasgow back to Girvan (the football season had finished), I found myself feeling depressed for two reasons.

Mrs Docherty had been her usual disagreeable self throughout my entire visit, despite my continued efforts to somehow ingratiate myself. Furthermore, Tommy was shortly scheduled to go to Canada with Celtic on an end-of-season tour. I didn't know for how long – I didn't ask because not seeing him for five and a half days a week had already proved difficult enough. But this young man had an inimitable way of lifting my spirits and he was about to surpass even himself.

That is probably why I can remember the following conversation verbatim. Without the slightest trace of warning, he turned towards me and said, 'When I get back from Canada next month, we'll get engaged and married very soon.'

As casually as I could manage, and also due to the fact that the two old ladies in the seat in front of us had abruptly stopped talking in their transparent anxiety to hear my response, I smiled and replied, 'Oh, we will, will we?'

He laughed out loud and said, 'Well, you *know* we will!' before pausing and then adding, 'Won't we?'

I was unable to disagree with him – nor would I have wanted to for a single second in case he should happen to change his mind.

His confidence wasn't born of arrogance, merely a quiet conviction. Although we had never even mentioned the subject until that moment, by then we both believed we were fated to be together and that our engagement was the next logical step towards a lifetime commitment.

Tommy was naturally disappointed when he discovered that he hadn't been chosen to go on Celtic's tour of North America that spring and, although I was similarly upset for him, I was also secretly delighted that he wouldn't be away for such a long time. Anyway, it was never in his nature to be dejected for longer than it would take for him to find a reason to be cheerful. It was just one of the many engaging traits of the boy I met and not, as I have also stated earlier, the man he would eventually become.

The following weekend resembled something from an early movie as, in that lovely old-fashioned manner that sadly seems to have been lost along the way with so many other worthwhile traditions, Tommy arrived to officially ask my dad for his eldest daughter's hand in marriage. I had decided to alert my parents of his intention on the Saturday morning, enabling Dad to consider his response.

After dispatching my brothers and sisters to random shops at the appropriate time, Mum's twitching ears joined mine on the pretext of looking busy in the adjoining kitchen while all my forewarned father had to do was lean against the fireplace in the living room, light his cigarette, listen intently, raise his eyebrow in feigned surprise and keep a straight face. There was never any question of Tommy's proposal being turned down, but my dad was a keen film fan and merely wanted to play out the scene correctly. I caught him peeking in the downstairs mirror several times that weekend, quietly convinced that he was Scotland's answer to Spencer Tracy. I always thought he looked a wee bit like him anyway.

Parental permission predictably granted, I caught the bus to Glasgow on Saturday, 11 June, where Tommy was waiting for me at St Enoch Square in the centre of the city. After much deliberation, and an equal amount of patience from the person hovering at my side, I eventually chose my diamond twist engagement ring at Samuels and we excitedly set the date for our marriage as Boxing Day, 1949. I didn't ask how he had been able to afford such a beautiful ring – I had been distracted by other jewellery when he bought it and assumed it could only have been on hire purchase – but it would have been ungracious to enquire anyway.

Then, bumping into numerous fellow pedestrians as I glided several inches above the pavement, glancing at the third finger on my left hand approximately every two seconds or so, Tommy transported me to a slightly higher level by happening to casually mention that Celtic were going to provide a rented flat for their promising young right-half and his new bride. I honestly didn't believe that anything or anybody could harm our future happiness. Well, I was wrong on that front. For one thing, Tommy had neglected so far to share our glad tidings with his mother.

When he did finally tell her, about five weeks later, Tommy arrived at our house clearly close to tears. Carrying all of his belongings in a weather-beaten brown suitcase, he explained to my parents that he had left home after a furious argument with his mother and asked if it would be okay if he stayed with us for a while. I could only imagine that Mrs Docherty was not exactly elated on hearing our news. Dad invited him in, Mum gave him a glass of lemonade, and then they both sent him straight back to Glasgow on the last bus to say sorry to his mother for losing his temper with her. When I nervously answered his call at the public call box the next evening, Tommy apologised for his unexpected appearance the day before but told me that his life at home had become unbearable. It seemed he had been constantly rowing with his mother and nothing he did was good enough for her.

I realised my mother had been absolutely right. It wasn't me that Mrs Docherty objected to; it would have been any girl Tommy intended to marry. I simply wanted her to be as pleased as everybody else and yet, to a certain degree and despite our strained relationship from the start, I could also sympathise with her. Her only son had been in the Middle East for two years and had no sooner returned home than here he was talking about going off and getting married to a wee lassie she barely knew. Yet I had always been counselled that it was better to release the chicks from the nest as soon as they feel ready. Let them go willingly and hopefully they'll return from time to time. As a mother in later life, it would prove to be sound advice for me.

To try to smooth things over, a few weeks later I suggested to Tommy that we postpone the wedding until his mother was more acquiescent. Not only did he flatly refuse to even contemplate any such delay, but my husband-to-be suggested that, by taking such a course of action, we would only encourage his mother to continue her personal crusade.

But as my restless nights evolved into indecisive days and Tommy continued to file frequent telephone reports from the Glasgow front line, I decided to regretfully raise the white flag. Totally alone in her opposition she may have been, but his mother's blessing was very important to my peace of mind.

Reluctantly, I realised I was never going to receive it so, towards the end of August, I sent my cherished engagement ring back to Tommy by registered post, together with a written apology, the fervent hope that he would understand and assurances that my love for him remained undiminished. Believe me, that precious piece of jewellery and the words that accompanied it were the most difficult items I ever placed in an envelope. In fact, it took me over half an hour to lick the stamps.

On receiving my letter, Tommy once again jumped on the next Girvan-bound bus and was back on my doorstep. Only this time, where before there had been the trace of tears, now there was only a shining determination and, smiling into those eyes, I immediately knew that, with the greatest respect, his mother had ceased to matter. We walked along the beach, talking, and, by the time we'd finished, our preparations for Monday, 26 December, were firmly back on track. We were going to be married!

CHAPTER 3

HEADING SOUTH

No, there's nothing half so sweet in life
As love's young dream.
THOMAS MOORE (1779–1852)

As the bitter winter of 1949 began to take hold, it was Mrs Thompson, our next-door neighbour, seeing me shivering patiently by the public call box at the end of the street on more than one occasion, who gave me her phone number and insisted that Tommy should call her house in future and she would come and fetch me. I was so grateful. My fiancé was not the most punctual person I had ever encountered. Sometimes he would call at about a quarter *past* nine and I once jokingly asked him if he had either forgotten or misheard the lyrics to one of our favourite songs.

At the end of October, almost a year since Tommy had first literally stumbled across my local dance floor, Mrs Thompson came round to tell me he had just rung and was on his way to Girvan. Apparently, he hadn't time to speak to me or tell her the purpose of his visit, only that he had to see me urgently. I imagined it must be to do with his mother and the wedding – and with that I could almost feel the colour drain from my face. Noticing my reaction, Mrs Thompson insisted that he had sounded thrilled and therefore surely it must be good news. I was not convinced, and spent what seemed like the next few hours nervously pacing the hallway and waiting not only for my fiancé but also my future to come knocking at the door. As soon as Tommy arrived, I saw that Mrs Thompson had been right.

He was quite breathless – having sprinted nearly two miles from the coach station – and between gasps for breath eventually blurted out that Celtic had accepted an offer of £2,000 for him from Preston North End and that (in those innocent, agent-free days) he had already agreed the terms and conditions and was going to be transferred at the end of the week. He told me that he had personally negotiated what was probably his new club's opening and closing offer – a salary of £8 a week during the season and £6 in the non-playing summer, plus a signing-on fee and bonuses of £2 for a win and £1 for a draw.

Back then, footballers were employed on annual contracts that ran from 1 July to 30 June. A player could re-register for the same club at any time between 1 April and the first Saturday in May. In effect, the rollover contract was simply reviewed and renewed every 12 months, even occasionally improved – always assuming, of course, that the club wished to retain his services at all. Tommy's agreement only differed in one respect. Because of the time of year, Preston had insisted on an eight-month contract through to the summer of 1950. Long-term security was measured in a matter of weeks, but I had sufficient faith in my fiancé's ability not to worry too much about something that I couldn't possibly have changed anyway.

By now, my parents had joined us in the hall – we hadn't managed to get any further into the house – and the three of us listened as he excitedly explained his reasons for accepting the transfer. Although he loved Celtic and always would, he said, and although Preston were only in the Second Division in England, having been relegated the previous season, they had started well and their team contained some established internationals. As a measure of their ambition, they had just broken the British transfer record by signing somebody called Eddie Quigley for £26,500 from Sheffield Wednesday. Playing in England and getting promoted would raise his profile, Tommy reasoned. It was a challenge that he wanted to take on, he said. I suppose Tommy never stopped looking for challenges of one kind or another throughout his life.

When he finally surfaced for air, Tommy looked at us and asked what we thought – despite the fact that he had already agreed to the move. I smiled apprehensively, knowing our lengthy discussions would come later, and looked at my dad. I saw him nodding approvingly, which I must admit surprised me given his lifelong allegiance to Celtic. Then my mum made us all roar with laughter by turning to me and saying, 'But, Agnes, that means you'll be going to live in *England*!' Bless her, you would have thought I was destined for the dark side of the moon. That said, I didn't have the remotest idea where to find Preston on the map and you may rightly wonder why I didn't immediately object to this major upheaval in my life without having first been consulted.

That's easy. I loved him. And if that meant moving to somewhere I hadn't even heard of that was fine by me. All that mattered was that I was with Tommy. I didn't know at the time, but such an adaptable attitude would stand me in good stead on the nomadic adventures that lay ahead of us. We were destined to move house about as frequently as some people go on holiday. Maybe more.

So, on 5 November 1949, Tommy was transferred to Preston and received a £300 signing-on fee. It was an enormous amount of money to us and we couldn't have wished for a better wedding present – until Tommy rang to inform me that we were going to have to postpone the wedding. On his first day training Tommy had looked at the fixture list and saw that Preston North End were due to play Sheffield United on 26 December. Our wedding day. He hadn't even known that teams in England played on Boxing Day. They didn't in Scotland. There didn't seem much point in Tommy asking his manager, Will Scott, for the day off so I attempted to pacify both of us by promising him that I would rearrange the wedding for as near the original date as possible. Having locked horns with his mother for so long and come this far, I certainly wasn't prepared to be beaten by Sheffield United!

Fortunately, changing the date was fairly straightforward, as 11:00 am the following morning was available. The most difficult part was carefully altering all the invitations with a steady hand to Tuesday, 27 December, but at least they hadn't already been posted. It proved to be a very early and valuable lesson in exactly where football would always reside on our list of priorities. Somewhere above second place. It was just as well that we did move the ceremony back by 24 hours, as my husband-in-waiting was picked for the Boxing Day fixture.

The club had offered Tommy a choice of two terraced houses at a subsidised rent of 15 shillings a week and he asked me to come and see which one I liked best. The long train journey south that Saturday in early December filled me with great excitement (I had never been over the border before) as did the thought of Tommy waiting for me at the other end. We were so happy to see one another and hugging him on the steam-filled platform made me feel as if I was part of some romantic wartime movie. He was in lodgings with a nice lady called Mrs Scott in Blackpool Road, Preston, no more than a five-minute walk from the football ground, Deepdale. I was also to stay there for the weekend, but as Tommy's landlady showed me to my room upstairs I suddenly realised I couldn't understand a single word she was saying.

By the time Tommy and I returned from a late-evening stroll, it had dawned on me that everybody in the town spoke exactly like Mrs Scott and I began to wonder if someone at the club could perhaps arrange Lancastrian lessons for me. I convinced myself that it couldn't be *that* difficult a language to learn.

As we travelled by train to spend the day in Blackpool on the Sunday morning, he noticed my worried expression and burst out laughing when I explained what was bothering me. For some reason it hadn't occurred to me but, of course, he had encountered the same problem when he'd first arrived in this curious country. Tommy's answer when confronted by the incomprehensible locals was to answer them back straight away in his own equally incomprehensible dialect. That way, both parties would be too

33

embarrassed to admit that they didn't understand each other and would pretend that everything was okay.

We went to see the two potential houses as arranged and I much preferred the first one, at 53 Lincoln Street. It was a two-bedroom terrace with a bathroom and an outside toilet. The property backed on to the railway shunting yard but, like Tommy's lodgings, it was only a short walk from Deepdale.

As I travelled back to Scotland that evening, I was thrilled at the prospect of the life that lay in front of me. I would soon be going back to stay in that strange land south of the border, as 27 December was just around the corner!

Unfortunately for Tommy, the same could hardly be said for travelling by public transport from Preston to Girvan after the match on Boxing Day, which North End won 4–1 on his home debut. It being a Bank Holiday, Tommy's journey to Scotland involved a long bus ride and several changes of train, culminating with him virtually sleepwalking into Mrs Thompson's house at 8:00 am on the morning of our wedding. He had been told to go next door as it was considered bad luck for the bride to see the groom before the ceremony. So much for superstition.

Our wedding was all I could have hoped and dreamed it would be. The church, Sacred Heart, was next door to where I had attended school and no more than a stone's throw from the Shelbourne Hotel where we had first met.

My dear cousin, Agnes Morgan (now MacNeill), was my chief bridesmaid, my two wee sisters, Mary and Margaret, and Tommy's youngest sister, Mary, were flower girls and his childhood friend, Jimmy Sheridan, was best man. Tommy and Jimmy in full flow could honestly have put Morecambe and

Wise out of showbusiness. My four brothers served the Nuptial Mass, so my parents had all of their seven children 'on view' at the service. Among the 150 guests I was glad to see Mrs Docherty, who attended despite her occasional threats not to. Tommy and I left a wonderful party in full swing to catch the 5:40 pm train for Glasgow. Even on my own wedding day I had to yet again leave while the music was still playing!

On our way to stay overnight at the Central Hotel, we were surprised to see our picture on the front page of the local evening paper. We laughed aloud when we realised it was a group photograph and our newfound 'fame' was due to so many far better-known Celtic players being at the lunchtime reception. The following morning, Tommy and I left to start our exciting new life together in Lancashire. I'm slightly embarrassed to tell it now, but before we left the hotel room I found myself glancing into the mirror several times to see if I looked in any way different now that I was a married woman.

Our first night in Lincoln Street was a glorious mess of clothes, presents and some second-hand furniture that my new husband had bought. While Tommy trained and tried to establish himself at the club, I happily set about making our house a home. Although it was almost always freezing – the toilet being in the back yard didn't help! – life was fun. You could almost touch the cold, but the constant laughter and love kept me warm. If there was ever any cloud on the horizon, it would have had a number nine on its back. That was the one I was living on. Every time he came home, the first thing Tommy did was to give me a huge hug and several kisses. I was even beginning to learn the local language. For instance, a wee currant loaf became a bun loaf, a pan was a pot and morning rolls were apparently something called baps.

Before our wedding, we had already received a wonderful early present on Christmas Eve, when my husband made his first-team debut away to Leeds United – on the left wing. Apart from suspensions, injuries and the fact they lost 3–1, I'm sure there must have been some method in the manager's madness, but it wouldn't be too long before Tommy made the right-half position his personal property. Anyway, they already had somebody who could play on either wing or at centre forward – anywhere, in fact, apart from goal. His name was Tom Finney.

To my mind, there was football and then there was Finney. He played the game with such grace, with a distinction that should embarrass many of today's prima donnas and I'm sure sadly doesn't. Let me enlighten you with some statistics regarding a player who spent his entire 14-year professional life (delayed by World War II) with his hometown club, Preston North End. Playing on either left or right wing or occasionally at centre forward, Tom scored 187 goals in 431 League appearances. In 76 internationals for England, he scored 30 times. With Stanley Matthews at outside-right and Finney on the opposite flank, England beat Portugal 10–0 in Lisbon in 1947, and Italy 4–0 in Turin 12 months later. Just imagine. On top of that, Tom was never cautioned. I put this down in part to his gentle nature, but also to the fact that, for eight seasons while Tommy played with him, Tom knew that any opponent who fouled him would be repaid in full by the young Scotsman playing directly behind him. It might take a few minutes or even six months, but Tommy Docherty would always exact a painful retribution for any offence committed on Tom Finney.

The late, great Liverpool manager Bill Shankly had preceded my husband as the North End right-half and he came to be a lifelong family friend – and football foe. I'll always remember the advice he gave to Tommy when the inevitable time came for 'Shanks' to bequeath his place in the team to the impatient pretender. Standing in the club dressing room, Bill threw his precious number four shirt across to Tommy and gently growled in his inimitable way, 'Just put it on, son. It runs about by itself.'

Bill couldn't possibly have known how right he would be. From first appearing in that position against Hull City at home on 4 March 1950, when they won 4–2, Tommy missed just one of the next 136 matches and that was only due to international duty. North End finished a distant sixth that season to the Second Division champions, Tottenham Hotspur, but we considered promotion to be a genuine possibility next time around.

Saturday was naturally the highlight of the week and a ritual for home matches was swiftly established. My husband would sleep until 10:30 am, when I would wake him and make a breakfast of bacon, toast and tea. While he was eating, I would prepare a steaming hot bath and, just before leaving to walk round the corner to Deepdale at 1:00 pm, he would drink a raw egg, mixed with milk, glucose and a liberal splash of dry sherry. The last vital ingredient was my dad's idea – he always maintained it improved the stamina. Little wonder that a rampaging young Scotsman snarling with venom and reeking of alcohol on a Saturday afternoon won far more tackles than he ever lost.

Christmas was seldom a family time in the house of a

professional footballer in the 1950s. Back then, they would often play home and away against the same team on 25 and 26 December. If the first fixture was away from home, North End would travel on Christmas Eve and, apart from watching him play the home fixture, I wouldn't see Tommy until Boxing Day evening. But we didn't mind. As our wedding anniversary fell on the following day, we tended to roll all of our celebrations into one delightful night.

Towards the end of that March, as Tommy began to cement his place in the team, I suspected I was pregnant but decided not to tell him as the doctor said that it was too early to confirm my condition. And then my early-morning-sickness routine was compounded by Tommy arriving back after training on the Thursday. He was ashen-faced as he sat down and whispered that something awful had happened. 'You've been dropped,' I said, imagining that to be the worst news he could possibly tell me.

'No,' he replied. 'I've lost my wages.'

Tommy had started off our married life by handing me his unopened pay packet every week. I didn't find this unusual, as I had grown up seeing my father do exactly the same. I don't know if it was a Scottish tradition or not – perhaps it was some method of evading responsibility? I remember asking him at various times in our early years to give me housekeeping money and see to everything else himself. The thought seemed to terrify him and he would ask for 'a few bob' and leave me to stretch the remaining amount as far as possible.

Anyway, we retraced his steps and even called at the police station, but nobody had handed the money in. We had drawn 0–0 at home to Plymouth Argyle the previous weekend, so there was also a £1 bonus. All £9 gone. Tommy had sent a third of his £300 registration fee to his mother in Glasgow and we had spent the rest on a double bed, three-piece suite, dining table and chairs, carpets, curtains and all the other items that go towards making a home. Now we were completely broke.

After frantically passing the afternoon looking and then soul-searching, he finally suggested that we should visit his 'uncle'. I had no idea who he was talking about. We wouldn't have dreamed of asking our parents for help – in the extremely unlikely event that they would have been able to – and I certainly didn't want to burden any other relative with our problem. But Tommy gently smiled for the first time in several hours and explained that, in Glasgow, 'uncle' was a euphemism for a pawnbroker.

In our desperation, we took a canteen of cutlery – an unused wedding present – to the pawnshop. Despite my intense embarrassment, I insisted on going in alone. I was worried that somebody would recognise my husband. I was in no mood to haggle with the stranger behind the counter and came out with just enough money to last until the end of the week, resolving never to go into one of those depressing places again.

The next day, a couple of hours before Tommy was due to travel to an away fixture at Chesterfield, Tom Finney called round to ask if I would like to stay over that night with his wife, Elsie, and their children. They had two-year-old Brian and a wee girl called Barbara, who had been born two days after our wedding. They lived in a beautiful semi-detached house and, at breakfast the next morning, Elsie innocently asked if I would like cream with my porridge. Perhaps it was an English custom, but *cream*! Elsie watched in bemused silence as I rushed past her and practically hurdled the furniture on my way to the bathroom, my morning sickness brought on by Elsie's unusual culinary offer.

There was great joy in certain households north and south of the border when our news became official, and we started to put Tommy's bonuses to one side so that we could afford to go back to Scotland for a holiday when the football season ended. My dad suggested that I should stay with them nearer the time the baby was due and, without saying a word in response, I had to smile at his badly hidden motive. He was a very proud, patriotic man and back then a boy could only represent the country of his birth at international football. He loved me too much to interfere, but I knew Dad didn't want to even *begin* to imagine the prospect of his grandson striding out one day to play for England!

For whatever reason, that conflict of national interests hadn't once entered Tommy's mind. He was anxious that I should have the baby at St Joseph's Hospital in Mount Street (the Finneys had recommended it), but it was privately run by nuns and would cost £20. Tommy didn't care about such extravagance. He was determined that our son – like my dad, he was utterly convinced it would be a boy – should be delivered as safely as possible. We began to put aside 10 shillings a week for that as well.

Fortunately, the team was reasonably successful so the bonuses became a fairly regular source of income. Because of our circumstances, every penny was always spoken for, yet we had everything we could have possibly wanted. Tommy loved playing more than anything, so when the close season arrived he was like a caged tiger. We travelled up to both Girvan and Glasgow by bus to visit my parents and his mother, but he hated the enforced period of inactivity. By the time pre-season training began in the middle of July, he was ready to be unleashed again.

It was during that time that I practically delivered our baby single-handedly. I had been given 25 October as the birth date, but on the day itself the baby showed no signs of coming. Bored and restless with waiting, I asked Tommy if we could go to the pictures. He didn't think it was a good idea, but I pointed out that the hospital was very close to the cinema and that we could take a suitcase with us in the event of my going into labour midway through the movie. As it was the night before payday, we only had three shillings left. The entrance fee to the cinema was about half that each, so we had no choice but to walk there and back. The average stay in hospital after childbirth then was about 10 days, so, by the time we arrived home at 10:30 pm, I think my husband was regretting his earlier insistence that we should take my heavy bag with us. He made me sit down and put my feet up while he went into the kitchen to prepare his *piece de resistance*.

I'll never know if it was nature or Tommy's beans on toast, but I went into labour just before midnight on Friday, 27 October. At 6:30 am I crept downstairs, not wanting to disturb Tommy, who had an important match that day at home to Sheffield United, the team that had caused the postponement of our wedding 10 months earlier. Finding me gone as he stirred in his sleep, Tommy came tearing downstairs at 8:00 am wearing thick pyjamas and the kind of panicked expression that only an expectant father can summon up.

I assured him I was fine and silently prayed that I could last at least until he left for the ground. He wouldn't hear of it. Tommy immediately took me into St Joseph's and our son was born at two minutes after midnight on Sunday, 29 October 1950. I had wanted to christen him either Matthew after my dad or Thomas after my husband, but Tommy insisted that we should name him Michael. He weighed precisely seven pounds and was the most beautiful thing I had seen in my entire life.

Tommy, being the over-excitable, hyperactive father-to-be that he was, had been sent out of the hospital to await the birth. So it was that, at about 12:15 am that night, he walked from our house to the corner of Lincoln Street to phone the hospital to see if there was any news. On being told that he was the father of a baby boy Tommy set about waking up the entire neighbourhood with his running, jumping and screaming. It was as though he had scored the winning goal in a Cup Final with the last kick of the game.

My father's reaction was, perhaps understandably, somewhat less enthusiastic. In his excitement, Tommy sent off telegrams to my parents and his mother. This was just five years after the end of the War and telegrams were still seen as harbingers of bad news. When the cable arrived at my parents' house, they were both anxious. Things went from bad to worse when Dad opened it, his face falling, as he exclaimed, 'Oh my God!'

Mum dropped the washing she was holding. 'What is it, Matt?' she pleaded with him.

Dad steeled himself to deliver the bad news: 'I'll tell you what it is – it's a boy. And he'll never wear a Scottish jersey…'

CHAPTER 4

GOOD TIMES,
BAD TIMES

If you can dream – and not make dreams your master,
If you can think – and not make thoughts your aim;
If you can meet with Triumph and Disaster
And treat those two impostors just the same...
RUDYARD KIPLING (1865–1936)

Michael was not only our perfect little boy, he also became our tiny talisman. Although money was in short supply, it would be wrong to suggest that we were exactly down on our luck before he arrived. However, we did occasionally wonder if he was some sort of lucky charm. I have heard of marriages where a baby invades a home and then slowly divides it. Michael merely augmented our love for one another. Of course, with an extra mouth to feed we were even more skint – another of my new words to place alongside bun loaves, pots and baps – and yet somehow it didn't seem to matter. We had each other – and our new son. And, within six months, Tommy would also proudly possess a Second Division championship winners' medal.

Probably through a mixture of luck, good judgement and general interference from the boardroom (in football, some things down the years have never changed), Will Scott, the North End manager, had assembled a marvellous young side that, even with a regular change at the helm, would virtually select itself for the next six or seven years and which went back up in considerable style at the end of the 1950/51 season, five points clear of runners-up Manchester City.

Yet, even with our new son to keep him occupied, the end of the football season saw Tommy as restless as ever to get back into the fray. Why kick your heels when you could be kicking someone else's? Friends told me that they'd seen him out on the streets, kicking pebbles around and playing pretend football, with a couple of lampposts for goals, such was his anxiety to get back to doing what he did best. He enjoyed playing games with his delightful wee boy, but now Tommy was desperate to play games against the *big* boys.

When the new campaign mercifully did get under way, the team quickly established itself in the First Division and Tommy's displays earned rave reviews in the local and occasionally national papers. The thought even crossed my mind that Tommy might one day be called up to the national side. However, I never mentioned it to anybody, least of all Tommy. The thought of him being chosen to represent his country... well, that was something that only ever happened to other, more fortunate people.

So was central heating. We had to make do with a back boiler, so, one bitterly cold evening (for a change) just after his first birthday, I was bathing Michael in front of the coal fire as

I usually did in the living room. Tommy was away training in nearby Morecambe with the team and then staying overnight. I had the radio on for company and was about to sponge my baby's curly blond hair when the presenter began to announce the Scotland side due to play Wales at Hampden Park in a Home International on Wednesday, 14 November 1951. I was only half-listening, but I could have sworn I heard him say, 'Docherty, Preston North End...'

My screams instantly drowned out the remaining names and Michael and I both burst out crying, him out of fear and me out of sheer joy!

Tommy had left a number where he could be contacted in case of an emergency. Although I assumed he must have heard the wonderful news himself, I decided to call Tommy anyway, to tell him how incredibly proud I was. I quickly dried Michael, wrapped him in several blankets and dashed round to use the phone at the corner shop. The line was permanently engaged and I suddenly suspected – oh, how I wished, hoped and prayed – that it was Tommy trying to get through to *me*. Sure enough, no sooner had I stopped calling than the phone started ringing. He was naturally ecstatic, told me how much he loved me and our son and asked me to promise him that I would take my dad to the match. I thought of my dear father back home in Scotland and smiled as wild horses started to gallop through my mind.

When Tommy arrived home the next day, we hugged, kissed and cavorted around the house several times before he told me a story that I found so hilarious it can still make me giggle over half a century later, despite everything that has since happened.

Stuart, one of Tommy's boyhood pals in Glasgow, had called the club that morning to congratulate him, and had happened to wonder, of course, if Tommy could spare him a couple of tickets for the game. He then told Tommy how he had heard the news.

Older readers, certainly in Scotland, will recall evening newspaper sellers in greatcoats and awful caps who used to stand outside stations and on busy street corners shouting out the two main headlines of the day as commuters barged past in their ill-mannered hurry to get home. There had been a terrible train crash that morning in which several passengers had lost their lives.

As he walked along Argyle Street on the approach to Glasgow's Central Station, Stuart first heard the cry from a distance. It seemed to him as if some prophet of doom was issuing a warning and that it was echoing across the grey, damp rooftops of Tommy's hometown. The old boy was shrieking: 'Disaster! Docherty picked for Scotland!' With tears of laughter obstructing his vision, Stuart finally managed to enter the terminal, only to hear another vendor calling out at the top of his gravelled voice: 'Docherty capped for Scotland! Tragedy!'

It was ironic that Wales would provide the opposition because Tommy hated the Welsh. He always has. I honestly never discovered the reason why and he would undoubtedly deny it until his face was the colour of the dark-blue Scottish jersey he walked out in on that unforgettable afternoon. But it's an unknown fact (until now) that could easily be substantiated by a patient football statistician. Just count the enormous number of players in the teams that Tommy selected at every club over his entire career as a manager and then tell me exactly how many of them were Welsh. I would be astounded if the number approached double figures. If Pele had been born in Prestatyn, Tommy would have dropped him for not scoring enough goals. Don't get me wrong, England are still the auld enemy but, for Tommy, they still had his respect. As far as he was concerned, the Welsh were worthy of nothing more than contempt. His sympathies lay with the Welsh poet Dylan Thomas, who remarked just before his death, 'The land of my fathers. My fathers can have it.'

My father and I were among the 71,270 other people at Hampden Park who watched Tommy stride out on to the pitch that day. It was then that I understood the true meaning of bursting with pride. As the national anthem began to play, I was aware of warm tears spilling down my cheeks. Dad glanced at me and asked what was wrong. 'I'm just so happy,' I answered. It didn't even bother me too much that Wales won 1–0. Tommy would have to wait almost exactly two and a half years to finally taste victory at international level, but, before any scornful assumptions are made about the quality of Scottish football either then or now, I must point out that it would be on only his fourth appearance due to both injury and the absence of today's meaningless friendlies.

Despite being knocked out of the FA Cup 2–0 in the third round by Bristol Rovers of the old Third Division (South) in the days when the lower reaches of the Football League were still regionalised, North End finished a creditable seventh in their first season back in the top flight, 11 points adrift of eventual champions Manchester United.

I suppose it was inevitable that our idyllic existence would take a severe buffeting at some point, but, when it did arrive, firstly towards and then at the very end of the following 1952/53 season, it was a double blow in the form of personal tragedy rapidly pursued by professional pain. On the evening of 4 February, I was seven months and contentedly pregnant again. Having drawn 2–2 at Deepdale, Tommy was playing at Spurs in an FA Cup fourth-round replay that night (they lost 1–0), but instead of putting my feet up as best I could – given that our two-year-old son was very ill with measles – I decided to move some bottled peaches and pears to the top shelf in our tiny walk-in larder. An urgent job, I know, and one for which I would never forgive myself.

Even by standing on a stool, I couldn't quite reach the highest point. And so, as I jumped up to try to put the first heavy jar on the shelf, I banged my head against the ceiling. I saw the proverbial stars and felt really queasy. Within an hour, I was suffering from such severe abdominal pain and obvious internal bleeding that I shouted through the front window to a passing neighbour to please fetch the doctor. He arrived within 20 minutes, administered an injection, ordered me to stay in bed and promised he would call back first thing in the morning.

That night was one of the longest and most traumatic of my young life. Michael had measles, my husband was in London and I was confined to a cold and lonely bed where, at just after midnight, I suffered a miscarriage. I prayed so very hard that I wouldn't, somehow always suspected I would and then crawled downstairs to the settee silently cursing my own stupidity. It was my worst living nightmare. When the doctor returned and surveyed the awful wreckage that I had been unable to face, he gently informed me that I would have had a son and wanted to immediately send for my husband.

I insisted he shouldn't be disturbed as Preston were travelling straight on to Cardiff for an important league game at the weekend. Thankfully, Michael had slept through the whole dreadful episode and, when Tommy returned late on the Saturday night (having won 2–0), it was to a very pale and distraught wife. I was heartbroken to have lost our baby and listened to myself softly crying an apology. As he held me tightly and tried in vain to comfort me, I wasn't aware that the large bump on my head would also be of great significance later in my life. After that terrible experience, I could never quite bring myself to smile at Bill Shankly's famous quote that 'Some people think football is a matter of life and death. I can assure them it is much more serious than that.' Of course, I recognised it as the typical exaggeration of a wonderful man – or, knowing him, was it?

Then, within two months, Tommy had to confront a completely different kind of despair as Preston finished runners-up on goal average to Arsenal in the race for the First Division championship. By 0.099 of a goal.

It is of little or no comfort, either, that, under the present rule of goal difference, Arsenal would *still* have won the title that season. The teams had finished level on 54 points from 42 games (both had won 21, drawn 12 and lost nine when a win was only worth two points), but the Gunners had scored 97 goals and conceded 64 (+33) while North End's return was 85 to 60 (+25). The convoluted system in those days meant that

Arsenal's goal average was recorded as 1.516 compared to Preston's 1.417. If you are waiting for me to explain the intricacies of the mathematical system involved, then please don't hold your breath because I was far from alone in failing to understand it.

Most people in *football* couldn't fathom it, so what chance did I have? All I know for certain is that I watched some of the greatest players in the world in my time but I never saw one of them who was capable of scoring 0.099 of a goal!

Off and on the pitch, in slightly less than three months, we had lost one of life's, and then one of the game's, greatest honours, but I was only ever inconsolable about one of them.

However, our collective spirits were marginally raised that springtime, when the club offered us a lovely semi-detached house at 20 Moorside Avenue, Ribbleton. The club's record signing, Eddie Quigley, had been living there but he was about to be transferred to Blackburn Rovers and we accepted without any hesitation. I was delighted that we would be moving for three specific reasons: the constant flurry of soot from the railway yard had become more annoying than I had originally anticipated, we would have the added luxury of an inside toilet – and I was anxious to leave the scene of my miscarriage as soon as possible. But then the pragmatist in me started to worry about the large increase in rent to £1 and five shillings a week. It was at this moment that Tommy suddenly decided his performances merited a substantial pay rise.

Now, the world of football has produced more than its fair share of apocryphal stories, but I can promise you that the following one is absolutely true.

Tommy arranged to meet North End's contracts manager on 20 April, armed with what he rightly considered to be two fairly powerful bargaining tools. Since his last deal, Tommy had become a permanent fixture in the first team and, of course, he was now an international. In fact, two days earlier, he had played in front of over 97,000 spectators at Wembley Stadium, when a last-minute equaliser from Lawrie Reilly of Hibs had secured Scotland a 2–2 draw.

Tommy had no specific figure in mind as he purposefully strolled to the ground that spring morning – just more than the amount the man in the dark suit and tie behind the desk was now proposing of £12 a week during the season, £10 in the summer and the same bonuses as before. On later hearing about it, I considered it to be a very generous offer, an increase of 50 per cent on his basic salary, but it wasn't nearly enough to pacify my husband. 'I know for a fact Tom Finney is on a lot more than that,' he argued, 'and I think I'm entitled to the same as him.'

The club official told him that was impossible, before adding, 'To be perfectly honest, Tom Finney's a better player than you will ever be.'

Even I, as biased a wife as you could ever wish to meet, would have had difficulty disagreeing with that observation, but Tommy still managed to have the last word as he sighed, signed and then stormed out of the office. His parting words were: 'Not in the bloody summer he isn't!'

Tommy made his third international appearance just over a fortnight later, losing 2–1 to Sweden at Hampden Park on 6 May, and returned home still complaining at the perceived injustice of his new contract at North End. But the improved terms enabled us to rent a television set, making us the envy of our neighbours. In an attempt to assuage my guilt regarding this ostentatious show of wealth, I invited the entire street round for a party to watch the Coronation of Queen Elizabeth II on 2 June. However, the new electronic gadget in the corner of the lounge backfired badly on my husband.

There was barely any football coverage at that time, but there seemed to be a surfeit of cricket due to a Test series between England and India that summer. Ted Fox, who lived three doors down, enjoyed the sport so much that he became a regular fixture in our lounge. Ted would come in and Tommy would automatically go out, sometimes into the back garden, telling me that he preferred to sit and watch the grass grow. Occasionally, in devilment and just before our neighbour expectantly arrived, Tommy would move the aerial to a point in the room where he knew it was impossible to receive a picture and Ted would trudge home, distraught that he had missed his white-flannelled heroes in action.

By the beginning of August, we were happily installed in our new home, Tommy, Michael and I – and, more often than not, Ted, who had quickly found his way to our change of address. Pre-season training had almost been completed when a car pulled up at the front gate. Neither we nor many of our friends owned a car and, looking out of the front window, I instinctively felt that something was wrong. I was correct. I saw George Bargh, the club physiotherapist, get out and open the back door. Out came a crutch, then another one, slowly followed by Tommy wearing an expression of complete disbelief on his face and a plaster cast on his left leg. I flew outside and we helped him into the house. He had broken a bone in his leg, just above the ankle. I could have cried for him. The first game of the new season was only four days away and now it looked as though he would be confined to the sidelines until Christmas at the earliest.

Nobody else had even been involved in the training-round accident. Apparently, Tommy had turned quickly in a practice match but the studs in his boot had stuck in the firm ground and prevented his foot from swivelling with the rest of his body. 'Mr Perpetual Motion' had been stopped in his tracks. In the coming weeks, the enforced physical inactivity made it difficult for him to sleep. He would while away the hours watching evening television – that's all that was generally available in those days – until the white dot faded to black and then slowly negotiate the stairs, step by step on his behind, to bed.

Tommy woke up one fitful night about a month after his injury, screaming in agony. I saw to my horror that his leg was so badly swollen that the skin was literally spilling over the plaster. I ran to the phone box in a blind panic and called Mr Bargh, before knocking on the door of my neighbour, Jean Green, and asking her to listen out for Michael in our absence. The club physio picked us up within minutes and drove straight to Preston Royal Infirmary, where they removed the cast with an electric saw, apologising that it had been set too tightly, before putting on a new one.

Tommy was playing again within 11 weeks. According to the medical prognosis, this was a remarkably short period. It didn't feel like it! With nothing on the TV and with no interest in reading, Tommy was constantly at a loose end. For something to do, we'd play cards in the morning, spend entire afternoons tackling jigsaw puzzles the size of small countries and then attempt to solve crosswords in the middle of the night.

By the time Tommy recovered, things were looking up. He went straight back into the first team – and I was pregnant again. North End's league form had been too erratic to sustain another title challenge and they finished in 11th position, with Wolverhampton Wanderers champions. People I spoke to in the town generally thought the team was suffering from a slump after the successes of the previous season. I preferred to blame it on the absence of their inspirational right-half for the opening 16 games of that campaign.

Tommy's left leg was noticeably thinner than his right when the plaster was removed but his stamina was improving almost daily. The trail that led every year to Wembley Stadium always began in early January and, by that time, Tommy had regained full match fitness. By 1 May 1954, proud Preston were in the FA Cup Final, against the League runners-up, West Bromwich Albion. To me, that was more than a mere coincidence. To back up my theory, the semi-final against Sheffield Wednesday at the neutral venue of Maine Road, Manchester, was a memorable match played in front of over 75,000 people. Charlie Wayman and Jimmy Baxter scored our goals in a comfortable 2–0 victory, but I believe that Tommy's contribution was equally crucial. Wednesday had an inside-forward called Jackie Sewell and everything revolved around him – until he was carried off on a stretcher after a crunching tackle by my husband. It was fair but it virtually cut Sewell in half. Although he managed to return to the fray, Sewell's heavily strapped leg meant he was little more than a passenger for the rest of the game.

The team had travelled down to London at the start of Cup Final week and the wives and families excitedly followed by special train from Preston on the Friday afternoon to stay at the Savoy Hotel. On the journey south, I was offered and accepted my first ever glass of champagne. I knew I shouldn't have done so in my condition but the atmosphere made me feel so decadent! My mum was surprised to learn that I had even intended to travel at all 'in your condition!' and Tommy had also been slightly hesitant. I appreciated they were concerned for me after my last pregnancy, but I replied that one was seldom given a second chance of being involved in a match of such magnitude. For his own peace of mind, Tommy offered our family doctor two complimentary tickets for the game in seats alongside me. It didn't require too much effort to persuade our football-mad, Preston-supporting GP to go into private practice for one day only.

On that subject, I remember Tommy returning from a match in London several weeks earlier and emptying the contents of his bag on to the bedspread. I hadn't seen so many 10-shilling notes since I'd worked as a teenage cashier at the Royal Bank of Scotland. I immediately realised that Tommy had sold some Cup Final tickets. I wasn't annoyed. I honestly believed the players in that era of the maximum wage were underpaid and, in any case, everybody accepted that it was one of the perks of getting to Wembley. What was more significant to me was that I stayed at a luxurious hotel. Of course, none of the wives, with the exception of Elsie Finney when her husband was on England duty, had ever stayed at the Savoy – or anywhere remotely like it.

I can smile now at the memory of how awkward and overwhelmed we all felt to be surrounded by such opulence. We hovered like a party of uninvited guests outside the daunting dining room before I finally said to nobody in particular, 'Look, I'm six months pregnant and both of us are starving!'

We all shuffled self-consciously to our seats and then discovered that every word of the menu was printed in French. No subtitles, just French. Fortunately, after several minutes of stunned silence, the waiter accurately assessed the situation and politely offered to translate.

Wembley Stadium on that particular Saturday in spring, with *your* team playing for *that* trophy in front of 100,000 spectators, was something I wish every supporter in the country could have experienced in those halcyon days. It was electrifying. There was such good humour. The teams were presented to Her Majesty Queen Elizabeth, The Queen Mother, everyone sang 'Abide With Me', I cried at the national anthem again – and then the game kicked off.

They scored through Ronnie Allen, but we equalised within a minute when a cross from Tommy was met by the head of Angus Morrison. Then Wayman put us ahead to maintain his record of scoring in every round. Then came the terrible turning point. Tommy was judged to have fouled Ray Barlow in the area and a penalty was awarded to WBA. Allen scored from the spot. 2–2. Then, with barely two minutes remaining, West Brom scored again through Frank Griffin. 3–2. Never believe anyone in football who says, 'Well, at least we got there.' You go there to *win*! And yet, in spite of that, I never once cried at the loss of a game of football, no matter how high the stakes.

I went back to the hotel and waited for Tommy and the rest of the team to arrive. After what seemed an eternity, Tommy finally walked into our room. He threw his runners-up medal violently across the room, telling me, 'I am going to *no* banquet down there tonight.' I watched the small case crash off the wall to the floor but didn't say anything. 'Did you hear me?' he demanded. In the days when supporters still took rattles to a match, he was clearly throwing his out of the pram.

I managed to brightly reply, 'I'm glad, my love, because I don't want to go either, looking like this.'

Suddenly his mood changed and he became attentive to my condition. I took the opportunity to tell Tommy that I didn't think it had been a penalty. He told me that, as he dejectedly boarded the team coach after the game, a drunken director had shouted out, 'Here he is, the fellow who lost us the Cup!' He was feeling guilty enough without that sort of stupid remark so I gently kissed him, quickly changed my mind and clothes and said, 'Come on, let's go and join the others. It will help you to get it out of your system.'

I was proved correct because, considering the general mood, it turned out to be a pleasant party and there was a beautiful black leather handbag at each lady's table setting, a gift from the club. Norman Wisdom and then The Bachelors performed in cabaret, closely followed on to the stage by my clearly rejuvenated husband and his impromptu rendition of a couple of slightly out-of-tune Sinatra songs. I think even Tommy and his unrivalled appetite for the game wouldn't have been too disappointed if the curtain had come down there and then on that eventful but empty-handed season. Domestically it had – the evidence of that being virtually the whole of Preston turning out to acclaim their vanquished heroes – but Tommy was leaving the next morning on international duty. He had been selected as the captain of Scotland for home and away friendlies against Norway, prior to playing in the World Cup Finals in Switzerland.

You may wonder why I haven't mentioned my husband's imminent appearance in football's most prestigious tournament in slightly louder and prouder tones. Well, apart from the fact he would yet again be away from home, there are two simple reasons. Before England hosted the event in 1966, when you may have heard anywhere but north of the border that they also won it, I genuinely don't believe the World Cup held the same global fascination that it has in modern-day football. Remember, there was minimal television coverage back then and not much more than results in the national newspapers. I remain convinced that it was only through the exploits of Bobby Moore and the boys of '66 that the tournament truly captured the imagination of Europe to become the worldwide phenomenon that exists today. The most accurate way to describe it way back in 1954 would be to compare it to the current African Nations Cup, an event of precious little interest outside that part of the world.

Secondly, without wishing to be condescending to that particular Scottish side, my husband wasn't used to playing in a mediocre team. As he told me himself, he expected to be 'home before the postcards'. Although in the build-up they beat Norway 1–0 at Hampden Park on 5 May, with a goal by Aberdeen's George Hamilton (Tommy's first international victory), and drew 1–1 in Oslo a fortnight later when John McKenzie of Partick Thistle scored, Scotland's subsequent World Cup adventure was indeed swifter than the Swiss postal service. After losing 1–0 to Austria in Zurich on 16 June, Scotland travelled to Basle three days later to face Uruguay, the reigning world champions, in a baking temperature far more suited to the South Americans and were thrashed 7–0. Disappointed, to say the least, Tommy still found time to joke that right-back Willie Cunningham, who also played alongside him at club level for Preston, had been run so ragged by the opposing left-winger that he was treated after the game for 'a sunburned tongue'.

Almost a year to the day since Tommy had broken his lower leg, it was once again my turn, albeit under far happier circumstances, to head for the hospital. I was grateful that we now had our own phone from which to call the local taxi company, because a young lady who would be christened Catherine Mary Docherty was in an awful hurry to enter this world. The cab arrived at midnight and our daughter was born at St Joseph's at 1:45 am on Saturday, 14 August 1954, weighing exactly nine pounds. She was an absolute beauty, with jet-black hair and eyes like enormous, dark saucers. Perhaps it's a peculiar thing to say, but I thoroughly enjoyed her birth. Maybe it was because she was so impatient to make her entrance or that I didn't feel at all tired and was therefore aware of the entire, magical procedure. I do know that it was just delightful to have a daughter. Tommy was the most attentive and tender of husbands and was equally thrilled to have a wee girl join our happy clan.

When I eventually returned home to our shining, flower-filled house, I remember thinking that everything was too perfect, surely it couldn't always be like this. It wasn't so much feminine intuition as a terrible premonition. In less than two months time, I was to discover how sadly correct I had been. My life would never be the same again.

CHAPTER 5

LOVE AND LOSS

No one ever told me that grief felt so like fear.

C.S. LEWIS (1898–1963)

Mum died from a cerebral haemorrhage in hospital on Sunday, 10 October 1954. She had just turned 54 and my own life turned totally upside down. It was an almighty blow and so hard to absorb. I don't know the exact time of her death – other than it being far too soon.

What *does* matter and what I *do* know is that she was deprived of her rightful pride of place at so many future family gatherings. Birthday parties, weddings and christenings that she would have cherished. I know she meant more than everything to me. I know she showered me with love and taught me things I didn't even know I was learning. And I know that, if I were to sit and stare at this particular paragraph for the rest of my own days, I would never be capable of adequately describing the enormous sense of loss I suffered or pay suitable tribute to her memory. So, as with life itself, I must move on. That much I also know.

In the days surrounding Catherine's birth, I had become increasingly concerned that I hadn't heard from Mum. She was far too thoughtful not to keep in touch, especially in the circumstances, but Tommy explained when he collected me and our brand new bundle on the Friday afternoon that my dad had called the night before to say one of my brothers had been ill with a throat infection. I later found out that this was a smokescreen. So, as soon as I had put my three children to bed (I always classed Tommy in that category the night before a match – in which they would beat Manchester City 5–0), I rang Dad. We were all nervously aware that Mum had suffered from high blood pressure for a long time – in fact, she had suffered two strokes in the previous five years – and yet he sounded fine, always a good sign I told myself, before he sweetly stumbled his way through an apology on her behalf and admitted that she was undergoing various tests in hospital.

It transpired that he had been under strict instructions not to worry me and I gratefully understood that I wasn't the only one carrying the emotional scars of my accident in the larder 18 months earlier. He added that Mum, no stranger to such tragedy after seven miscarriages of her own, merely required a prolonged rest. But, when she failed to reply to the letters that I was now writing every other day, I feared the worst. I hope it's my imagination, but I've often wondered whether Dad's choice of the words 'prolonged rest' were his way of trying to tell me one of the last things I could ever wish to hear.

If solace can ever truly be found in the death of a loved one, then, in Mum's case, it means that, when she walks and laughs through my dreams, as she so often does, she is forever young.

And yet there I was, suddenly back in the future and only two years younger than she was when she died, listening to my husband's pointless pleading half a lifetime later.

While I prepared to make the painful journey back up to Girvan, Tommy was faced with a dilemma. He had been selected to represent Scotland against Wales at Ninian Park, Cardiff, the following weekend but had to join up with the rest of the squad on Wednesday, 13 October – the day of Mum's funeral. I can't remember who once said that death is no respecter of age but football clearly cares even less for families. First my wedding and now this unforgivable intrusion. I made a mental note never to organise a function for any Wednesday, any weekend or any time around Christmas ever again. The thought occurs to me now that, if televised sport had existed then as it does today, we may never have confidently arranged any single occasion in our lives together.

However, I had no hesitation in telling him that he must travel and Dad supported me by saying it was the way Mum would have wanted it. In fairness, Tommy was genuinely prepared to phone the Scottish Football Association and withdraw from the team on compassionate grounds but I knew in his heart, and in spite of the fact that he loved my mum very much, he was desperate to play. He was always desperate to play. What I couldn't have foreseen was just how much I was going to need my husband's support on that dreadful day. So Tommy went west to his least favourite place on the planet (where they won 1–0 with a goal from Paddy Buckley of Aberdeen) while my brother John and his new wife Margaret, who had moved to Preston, helped me travel north with my two wee children to confront one of the saddest occasions of my life.

I was so distressed in the middle of the crowded Requiem Mass that I left my children with random relatives and found myself running blindly back to 58 Bourtreehall, the house of my childhood. I don't know for how long I stood on that street, staring at the tiny corner property where so many memories lived. It was a home haunted by happiness. I didn't feel that I was being disrespectful by leaving the church because, traditionally, women didn't go to the cemetery in those days anyway. It was always left to the men to solemnly walk behind the cortege to the burial ground.

That afternoon, and I'm certain as a direct result of my overwhelming grief, I discovered my milk had dried up and I was unable to breastfeed Catherine. Yet, almost unbelievably, I found myself smiling as I listened to countless aunts and female family friends respectfully whispering that their own recipe of solid food was the correct one for my baby. Some of them were even spinsters but that didn't prevent them from having a forceful opinion. Every funeral should have a baby in the house afterwards. They not only provide hope for the future but also, far more pertinently, distraction.

Tommy and I had previously agreed that the children and I should remain in Girvan for the following fortnight to help my distraught dad look after my 10-year-old brother, James, and sisters Margaret (12) and Mary (17) in an attempt to establish some kind of simple domestic pattern for their future. But it was hopeless. I quickly realised the poor man couldn't contemplate anything beyond the burning end of his latest cigarette. He was bewildered and, most worrying of all, his condition seemed to visibly deteriorate with each passing day. Unable to eat, drink or sleep, all he could do was chain smoke and cry. Whereas before he had always been contentedly quiet, now he was simply dumbfounded. Mum seemed to have taken his spirit with her and I was frightened that he would be incapable of looking after himself, let alone three children.

When I returned to England I immediately voiced my deep concern to Tommy and we decided that the best, the only, solution would be to move all of them to their own house in Preston. We clearly didn't have the space but fortunately, for the first time in our lives, we were in a financial position to be able to relocate them. Not only was Tommy playing reasonably regularly at international level but he had also just received his loyalty payment of £750 that winter for five years' service to North End. It was known as a 'benefit', a sort of semi-testimonial, and amounted to £499 after tax.

He had already bought a second-hand soft-top Morris Minor, which he proudly and erratically drove around town for quite some time before finally passing his test, and we used the rest of the money as a deposit for 8 Rook Street. The house was in Tommy's name with a mortgage which Dad would repay in the form of monthly rent. They moved in at the beginning of February 1955, and Dad quickly found a night job cleaning offices.

Our dreams of an immediate return to Wembley were extinguished the following evening. Having earlier drawn 3–3 at home against Sunderland in the fourth round of the FA Cup, North End lost the replay 2–0 on 2 February. However, exactly two months later, Tommy was back at the famous old stadium – and probably wishing that on this occasion he had withdrawn from the national team. He scored the final goal of the game in the 85th minute against England at Wembley Stadium – his solitary goal for his country in what would be a 25-cap career. Was this a cause for celebration? Hardly. By the time Tommy scored, England were already 7–1 up. With Tommy's contribution, the game ended 7–2 to the auld enemy.

That was also the match in which a Manchester United wing-half made his international debut and became the youngest player at that time to ever represent England. He was just 18 years old and his name was Duncan Edwards.

Almost a year before the loyalty award became due, we happened to notice a newsagents-cum-post office that was up for sale. It only came to our attention because it was virtually on the doorstep of Deepdale. Tommy had started to coach schoolboys on several afternoons a week across Lancashire but it was strictly on an expenses-only basis and we thought that acquiring the business would provide financial security towards an uncertain future when his playing days were over. The problem was that we needed £600 as a deposit. Tommy asked the club if it would be possible to receive his benefit money in advance but they flatly refused. Had Preston been more helpful, we would have bought the shop and would therefore have been unable to afford to transport my grieving father, younger brother and sisters to England.

My dad had arrived as a clearly grateful and yet reluctant immigrant and my heart went out to him. In the space of less than four months, that gentle little man had lost the only woman he had ever loved and left the only country he had ever known. But I simply had to have him near me. He needed protection. I did too. Dad's arrival kicked off the most hectic time of my life.

For the rest of that season, in which North End finished in a disappointing 14th position behind the champions, Chelsea, and into the 1955/56 campaign, I somehow succeeded in looking after Tommy and our children, Dad and his equally chaotic household, passed my driving test and then discovered that I was pregnant again. I'll never know where I found the time – certainly for the last of those events! But I was young, healthy and so much in love.

I also seemed to have unwittingly adopted the role of part-time landlady for any North End players whose wives were about to have babies. Obviously incapable of feeding themselves, they would aimlessly wander back with Tommy after training for their lunch. It was an unspoken agreement that they would arrive and I would automatically cook. Among them, Fred Else had the majority of his meals with us while Marjorie was in hospital expecting their first child. He caused much hilarity when he offered to help with the washing up and dropped two of the first three plates that I handed him to dry. He was our goalkeeper!

Frank O'Farrell was also a regular visitor under the same circumstances, although his dear wife, Anne, had a stillborn baby. I even looked after their eldest daughter, Bernadette, at our house for several days as Anne was kept in Preston Royal Infirmary for observation. The canteen that my kitchen quickly became was to stand me in good stead because, as if all of that wasn't enough, we were about to go into a joint business venture running a café in the town centre with another Preston player, Joe Dunne.

Within the first week of taking over the Olympic Café, I realised how fortunate I was to have 'inherited' Winnie, Teresa and Margaret. Especially Margaret. The first two ladies were friendly, experienced waitresses who had happily agreed to continue working under the new and extremely naive management and the third and considerably younger lady was my wee sister, my built-in babysitter, who possessed the patience of a saint. With Catherine, she required every ounce of it. I know my lovely daughter will forgive me but, in one crucial respect, she was the most awful baby imaginable. Perhaps it was the abrupt change to her diet when she was only eight weeks old but that little madam never slept through one single night. Ever. Her contented snores were merely a pleasant prelude to the storm and, when it inevitably broke, Margaret was generally there to slowly stem the downpour while I worked endless hours in the café.

I started my catering career by providing a businessman's lunch for 3/6d and we had an average turnover of 100 meals per day. It may sound a lot but there was only a marginal profit in that particular part of the business. However, we more than made up for it in the evenings, with youngsters buying large Cokes and simple sandwiches and the place rapidly grew in popularity.

That was no great surprise, because whenever Preston played at home Tommy and Joe would spend most of the evening shaking hands, signing autographs and discussing that day's game with the supporters. Many of the other players, including

Tom Finney, Fred Else and Willie Cunningham, would often drop in and join the impromptu debate.

Win, lose or draw, my husband was in his element. As you can imagine, word spread as quickly as the butter on the bread, for, although we had no alcohol licence, the chance for a fan to simultaneously feed his face and his football habit guaranteed a full house. Suspiciously, though, if North End were playing *away*, Tommy and Joe never seemed to manage to get back until the moment the final clean plate was being safely stored away. I could easily understand that when they had been at, say, Arsenal or Newcastle. It was slightly harder to stomach when the match was at Bolton or Blackpool.

Speaking of stomachs, mine was becoming considerably larger. To the point where, on reflection, I was nothing short of stupid. The nearby Queens Hall hosted Big Band Nights most Saturdays and I decided to put in a tender to the local council to cater for the audience. We were awarded the contract to sell filled rolls, meat pies and soft drinks to the public, while the likes of Joe Loss and his Orchestra and Johnny Dankworth and Cleo Laine performed. It had taken me until almost the age of 27 but I had finally succeeded in staying until the music stopped – except I was dancing and simultaneously serving behind the counter with Winnie and Teresa.

I appreciate now that getting home at midnight to do the accounts, wash tablecloths, iron them two hours later and then see to Catherine when she chose to erupt wasn't a very sensible way to behave for a woman who had suffered a miscarriage exactly three years earlier and who was now four months pregnant. And, one night in the early February of 1956, nature arrived to teach me a severe lesson. I was slowly lowering the roof that my daughter had once again raised when I discovered to my horror that I was bleeding quite badly. I woke Tommy and he called the doctor. I was admitted to Preston Royal Infirmary within the hour and told that I would definitely lose my baby. I spent seven long days confined to bed in that hospital and, call it willpower, bloody-mindedness or whatever you want, but I prayed myself prayerless, tried to stay awake in case my body did something untoward when I inevitably drifted to sleep and refused to even consider the prospect of losing another child.

I can only thank God I didn't and my lovely son, Thomas (I finally had my own way on that Christian name!), was eventually born on Tuesday, 17 July, at 5:25 pm in St Joseph's Hospital. Completely unlike his sister, he was in no great hurry to enter this vale of tears and kept me in labour for more than 24 hours. He weighed 7 lbs 6 oz and was the most beautiful baby boy. But his birth should have served as a warning, because he has generally been late all of his life.

In most people, I would find it annoying, but in Tom, as he naturally came to be called to avoid confusion, I have always found it endearing. In later life, as I proudly watched him grow, he has always reminded me of my father in that he is not only a gentleman, he is also a gentle man.

I arrived home to discover that my first son Michael had fallen head over heels in love with a considerably older woman. We all knew it couldn't last, if only because of the age difference. He wasn't quite six years old and Mrs O'Neill was his first schoolteacher at the Blessed Sacrament in Ribbleton.

She had come to the house just after my stay in hospital to see if anything was wrong and told me, 'The light has gone out of Michael's eyes.'

I realised the true extent of Michael's devotion to her when my engagement ring disappeared. I searched the entire house for that irreplaceable piece of jewellery, the ring I had regretfully placed in an envelope some seven summers since, wondering all the time how I would be able to tell Tommy that I had lost it. I had virtually given up hope and started to prepare Michael's clothes for school the next day when I found it in the right-hand pocket of his short trousers. He explained that he had seen it on the side by the sink while I had been washing up and thought 'it was so pretty and shiny that I wanted to show it to Mrs O'Neill'. Bless him.

At some point during that summer, Tommy became TD and I therefore naturally started answering to the initials of AD. He had also, on one of my trips to the finger-wagging, imaginary soapbox that I occasionally climbed on to, christened me 'The Wee Yin', many years before Billy Connolly emerged from Tommy's birthplace as the bigger variety. TD was even more restless than usual and decided the solution was to ask for a transfer.

Unlike his move from Celtic, he had deigned to discuss his thoughts with me this time and I could appreciate his motives. He didn't have anywhere else to go, he just didn't want to stay there. He was 28 years old and an established international, but a footballer's career didn't last nearly as long then as it does today.

So he reasoned – rightly, I thought – that Preston were probably never going to win anything and a move to a more successful club while he was still in his prime would enhance both his medal-winning prospects and our bank balance. Definitely in that order. Ask any committed professional footballer, even today I like to think, and they would promise you the same. They would take a pay cut in exchange for trophies. It's the competitor in them.

His decision created headlines in the newspapers and Tom Finney called round, pleading with him to 'settle down'. North End had finished 19th at the end of the previous season, narrowly avoiding relegation by a single point and had been unceremoniously dumped out of the FA Cup 5–2 at West Ham United in the third round. Not surprisingly, the board refused to grant Tommy's request and, I'm almost certain by way of appeasement, offered us a beautiful detached house with parquet floors to rent at £1 and 15 shillings a week at 94 Cromwell Road. It became our home for the next two years before we finally did leave Lancashire.

The following campaign, in which Preston finished eight points and third behind champions Manchester United and level on points with runners-up Tottenham Hotspur, merely confirmed Tommy's suspicions. He wasn't particularly unhappy, he was just frustrated at being the perennial bridesmaid. A 2–1 defeat at Arsenal in an FA Cup fifth-round replay hadn't exactly helped. Tommy sold his share in the café to Joe Dunne in the early summer of 1957 as part of his continuing determination to leave Preston. He was also concerned that the late nights may have been affecting his form. I missed working there at first, but my husband and three young children were more than enough to keep me occupied.

At the start of July, we had arranged to visit Ray and Monica

McLoughlin, some friends who had moved to Howth, just outside Dublin. When the time came I was unwilling to leave the children and nervous about flying for the first time, but I went anyway. My brother John and his wife looked after my baby, Tom, while Tommy's mother came down to stay at our house with Michael and Catherine with my sister, Margaret, helping out. It was wonderful to be away with my husband on our own and the weather was glorious. Ray and Monica were terrific company, while also affording us our own space, and we didn't seem to stop laughing for the entire week.

It was just as well that I had recharged my batteries because within days of returning, and although all of my children were immunised, Catherine developed whooping cough and Tom quickly followed suit. It was a very frightening and wearing time for me but I nursed them back to health through endless nights as their father soundly slept along the hallway.

I was thankful that my frequent trips to and from their bedrooms didn't appear to disturb him as he had to maintain his levels of fitness, but he did notice me returning on one occasion. It was just after 3:30 am as he rolled over and whispered, 'You look just like Florence Nightingale – only with a torch' and went straight back to sleep. But no sooner had I seemed to blink than the new season was under way – and North End were playing some fantastic football.

And then came Thursday, 6 February 1958. A date forever ingrained in the minds of football people of a certain age everywhere.

Tommy had spent the early part of that afternoon coaching some schoolboys in Orrell, near Wigan. His total commitment to the game had already made me appreciate that half-heartedly running some café or post office in Preston for the rest of his days would always be a poor substitute for his first and enduring love. He never loved anything as much as he loved the game. I remember well one of Tommy's earliest interviews. When asked what hobbies he had, he thought for less than a second and replied, 'Football.' Tommy could never have composed a speech to save his life, but he was fluent in football and confident enough to transmit his ideas to hungry youngsters. It was only when he arrived home just before teatime and failed to mention anything in particular that I realised he couldn't have possibly heard the terrible news. I had to first tell him – and then watch him sit quietly by both the television and radio as the nightmare of that day slowly unfurled.

That was the first time I saw my husband openly cry. I had seen him close to tears on my parents' doorstep nearly a decade earlier, when his mother had tried and failed to sabotage our impending marriage, when he had lost the FA Cup Final and when he had first held his newborn children. But this was savagely different. This was the Munich air disaster, the pointless loss of so much potential, the almost total destruction of a memorable Manchester United team lovingly nurtured by their manager, Matt Busby. Nobody will sadly ever know what they might have achieved and most people today are too young to have ever witnessed them in action.

Tommy had played against the young men who died in that terrible plane crash so many times and had been left literally breathless by their ability. From his earliest days as a coach and manager, he was inspired by the very concept of the Busby

Babes. Many years later, Matt Busby (who refused to have us call him Sir Matt, saying it made him feel uncomfortable, 'like some headmaster, demanding respect rather than earning it') mentioned to me that he had always hated the Busby Babes sobriquet, believing that the reference to youth somehow suggested a sign of weakness that he felt did not exist in that group of men. It's no secret that he chose to carry the guilt of their deaths for the rest of his life.

I recall watching a television documentary called *REUNITED* that my son, Tom, produced and directed 35 years later. It was made in 1993 to celebrate the 25th anniversary of United's 4–1 European Cup Final triumph against Benfica at Wembley on 29 May 1968, but, without exception and totally unprompted, every single one of those players spoke of a sense of destiny, of honouring the players who had died a decade earlier at Munich and of winning that elusive trophy for Matt and the young men who didn't make it.

In particular, I listened to Bill Foulkes define the grief that I know he will carry to his own dying day. These are the eloquent words from that programme of the United centre-half, one of the few to miraculously survive the tragedy: 'They were all friends of mine and I can see them now. I see them every day. I never forget their names or their faces. They're clear – in fact they get clearer every day. There's nothing sad or morose about it now. It's just great that we did justice to their memory.'

Such a heartfelt tribute makes it insensitive to single out any individual who lost their life as a result of that crash, so please forgive me but I do remember Tommy telling me that, along with Tom Finney, Duncan Edwards was the closest he ever witnessed to the complete player. He would probably have captained England in the 1966 World Cup if he hadn't died at the tragically tender age of 21.

Even today, when I occasionally listen to a sports reporter describe a missed putt or dropped catch as a 'tragedy', I find myself squirming and remembering Munich. I used the word once before and I'll revisit it on several more occasions in the course of this book. Perspective.

Here's another one. Parsimony. I have no wish to appear controversial or to denigrate the memory of such a marvellous man, but the Scots are – how can I delicately put this as one myself – somewhat renowned for their financial prudence, and Matt Busby was nobody's fool. Of course he had a vision of vibrancy, of a young and exciting team who could outpace and outplay any opposition, and I'm certain that his fantasy became a major factor in Tommy's future career in coaching and management. But Matt also knew the natural exuberance of youth meant that, in the era of the maximum wage, those young men were almost prepared to play for nothing. And so they almost did. In return, United received the optimum output for the minimum of outlay. Until most of those boys paid the ultimate price in Munich. Some years later, although to a naturally far less significant degree, that German city would come back to haunt me as well.

Just over two months after the tragedy, on 19 April to be precise, Tommy captained his country against England at Hampden Park in front of 127,874 spectators and lost 4–0. Astonishingly, after crawling from the wreckage that claimed the lives of so many of his colleagues and close friends, United's

Bobby Charlton was one of the scorers on his international debut – from a cross by Tom Finney. But I think that even proud and patriotic Scottish hearts and minds didn't particularly care that day. For the most committed players and fans alike, events can sometimes supersede sport. That was such a day.

I also believe that it understandably caused TD to become all the more determined to make the most of his own remaining days as a player. The same reflective mood seemed to affect his manager and board of directors because, in August 1958, and with the whole of sport still stunned by the disaster, Tommy was finally granted his transfer request.

Or, if I'm being cynical, and God knows after so many years in the game I feel entitled to be, maybe they thought he was approaching his sell-by date. They couldn't have been more wrong. Once again, Preston had finished the campaign as runners-up – this time five points adrift of Wolverhampton Wanderers – having scored exactly 100 goals in the process. Their FA Cup exit in the third round, 3–0 at home to our local rivals and eventual winners, Bolton Wanderers, hardly eased the frustration of yet another empty-handed season. If football then was how it is today, consolation could have been found in qualifying for one of Europe's major competitions. But back then, you were either first or nowhere. Some would argue that's the way it should still be. To me, and I know that I'm far from alone, qualification to the Champions League for finishing fourth domestically seems to be a slight contradiction in terms.

Anyway, Tommy had returned from Scotland's latest and predictably brief World Cup adventure in Sweden, where they drew 1–1 with Yugoslavia and lost 3–2 to Paraguay and 2–1 to France and, after once again waiting for his own postcards to arrive, had been expecting to join Preston on their pre-season tour of South Africa. The manager was now Cliff Britton and, when we discovered Tommy hadn't even been invited on the trip, I was put in charge of drafting his next transfer request. He was so furious that I swear he would have refused to start the season for them. Fortunately, it didn't come to that, yet I was still one of the last to know what was looming on the horizon – and not for the last time either.

North End were playing Arsenal at home on 23 August, the opening day of the 1958/59 season, and as I was dashing to get ready for the game I heard on the radio that Tommy had signed for Arsenal for £30,000 and therefore, due to an obvious conflict of interests, he wouldn't be playing that afternoon. He didn't appreciate the power of the media at the time – although he would more than make up for that in the years to come – and later explained he was going to tell me after the match. I wasn't at all annoyed. Instead, I watched Preston win 2–1 with mixed emotions, walked home, picked up the phone and called my friends at Pickfords while my recharged husband prepared to remove himself ahead of us to London for the next step on our odyssey.

CHAPTER 6

CAPITAL GAINS

When a man is tired of London, he is tired of life.
SAMUEL JOHNSON (1709–84)

With its famous marble entrance hall at its old ground at Highbury, Arsenal Football Club has always been regarded as one of the most sedate and respected bastions of the English sporting establishment, leading me to suspect that they were totally unprepared for the arrival of my vociferous husband.

We now live in an age of strategically placed microphones in televised sport, but back then I would often sit in the company of countless thousands of screaming spectators and clearly be able to hear Tommy swear at, encourage, berate or cajole his colleagues. In fact, it was mostly just swear. He never swore at home but more than made up for it on his field of dreams.

Whether Arsenal was ready for him or not, I was more than ready for London. My only previous glimpse had been that weekend of the 1954 FA Cup Final and I had been mesmerised by the sheer energy of the capital. The West End theatres, shops and restaurants were particularly appealing now that TD's salary had 'rocketed' to £17 a week, £15 in the summer, and £2 for a win and £1 for a draw.

Of course, nobody knew at the time that this was a city on the edge of social and cultural revolution. Of Mary Quant and mini-skirts, Twiggy and Mini cars, Carnaby Street, flower power and flared trousers. The decade that would be dubbed and forever remembered as the Swinging Sixties – and I was about to be transplanted into the very heart of it from placid Preston. Michael Caine as Alfie might have known what it was all about, but quantum leaps didn't come much higher for me.

The club provided a rented house for us at 4 Ashurst Road, Cockfosters, Hertfordshire, about 20 minutes by tube from their training ground. Although the property was slightly smaller than our previous place in Preston, it didn't matter. What mattered after taking almost five weeks to sort everything out was that we were all together again. In fact, as I was still arranging our move from Lancashire, Tommy made his debut for the Gunners. That same day back in Preston I had taken the children out for an evening walk to the newsagents. While in the shop, I peered at the stop-press column over a man's unsuspecting shoulder to find out North End's result. It was only when we were roughly 200 yards back down the street that I realised I had looked up the wrong team! Having admitted that, I should tell you there is no more fickle person on this planet than a footballer's wife. Her allegiance has to alter quite literally overnight. I read recently that you don't choose your football team, it chooses you. That may well be true but a footballer's wife is the exception to the rule.

TD had travelled up from London to drive us back down to our new home and was so enthusiastic about his new team and surroundings that I was unable to get a word in edgeways. He was now 30 and this would be his last realistic tilt at a major trophy as a player. He had high hopes, because Arsenal and Manchester United were the two dominant forces in English football.

However, Tommy's first two seasons as an adopted Gunner ended in the kind of disappointment he had reluctantly grown accustomed to during his days at Preston. In the 1958/59 season, they were knocked out of the FA Cup 3–0 in a fifth-round replay by Sheffield United (yes, that team again!) and finished a distant 11 points and third in the League behind champions Wolves and Manchester United.

On 11 April, just before his 31st birthday, Tommy made what would be his final international appearance. He was back at Wembley and again it ended in defeat, Bobby Charlton scoring the only goal of the game. It was also the day that the English captain Billy Wright became the first player in the world to win 100 caps.

The following year saw Arsenal beaten 2–0 in the third round by Second Division Rotherham United (of whom more later) in a second Cup replay and end up a lowly 13th in the table to the champions Burnley. Yet, for all that, we were still thoroughly enjoying the new experience. I was fortunate over those nomadic years that the children seemed to have inherited my ability to adjust to new surroundings and, in their case, schools. They all made friends easily but that came as no surprise to me. If I had been a child, I would have wanted to know them as well.

Michael quickly settled in at his new school, St Monica's in Southgate, North London, but Tommy's career, of course, remained the fulcrum of our family life and he often told me how important a part I played in the process. It never occurred to me to question his movements. If he said he was going to a game on any given night of the week, why would I have checked the paper for the fixtures? Is there something so wrong in just being there for someone you love and trust? He used to say he had 'the best digs and the best landlady in the world' and, in retrospect and with due modesty, he was absolutely right.

He led a bachelor existence that enabled him to concentrate completely on his job. I wouldn't have had it any other way but I genuinely didn't think I had anything to worry about in those days regarding other women. I never spared a second thought – or a first one for that matter – on such possibilities. We were extremely happy together and had three gorgeous, healthy children. Money continued to be tight, if not more so now that we were living in London, but men surely can't conduct extramarital affairs when every penny is needed at home for family purposes. Can they?

Knowing him and his deceptive ways as well as I unfortunately do now, perhaps they can, but back then I only have fond memories of a man who, on a weekly basis, would take the children and I to the Cartoon Theatre in Leicester Square and demand to stay second time around, roaring with laughter the whole way through. I swear he would have stamped his feet and had a public tantrum if I hadn't agreed

JUNE 19, 1977   No. 4980   12p   Ls

THE DOC RUNS OFF WITH TEAM WIFE

TOMMY Docherty's marriage is on the rocks. He has fallen for a woman 18 years his junior.

The controversial Scots manager of Manchester United has walked out on his wife, Agnes.

He plans to start a new life with the wife of the club's first-team physiotherapist.

She is Mary Brown, 31, whose husband Laurie was already with the club when Docherty took over United four-and-a-half years ago. The Browns have two daughters.

Last night Docherty, 49, wed 27 years and soon to become a grandad for the third time, spoke of his affair.

He said in an exclusive interview: "We are in love. We've got something special going for us and we've decided we would like to spend our future together.

"We haven't rushed into this. There's been a lot of soul-searching.

"The bond has grown between us over the last three years, and we've decided to bring this relationship out in the open rather than live a lie.

Meeting

"Mary and I plan to set up home together and hope eventually to wed."

He told Agnes of our decision and Mary has told Laurie.

"I believe that what has happened between Mary and me will be understood and accepted. It happens, after all, to other people every day."

Docherty, who has four children — the youngest 11, the eldest 25—said that as far as he is concerned his position as manager of the English F.A. Cup-holders is not affected.

"This has nothing at all to do with football," he went on. "It is a private matter and I've always believed in keeping my public and private lives separate.

"I shall continue to devote my time to keeping United a top team."

The United directors have been told of the situation and are expected to hold an emergency meeting to discuss whether any action should be taken.

The Browns' children, aged seven and four, are with their father in Manchester.

Late last night Laurie Brown, one of

By Sunday People Reporter

Docherty's best friends, was close to tears as he spoke about the revelation of his wife's love affair with his boss.

"What can I say? I just hope it's not true— that's all," he said.

Asked where he thought the revelations had come from he said: "It must be the boss ... It must be."

About his future with Manchester United he said: "After this—what future?"

Docherty, born in the East End of Glasgow, has frequently hit the headlines with his outspoken views and no-nonsense decisions with players and clubs' managements.

He played for four League clubs, captained Scotland in the course of winning 25 caps, and gained a Cup runners-up medal in 1954.

He has managed Chelsea, Rotherham, Queen's Park Rangers, Aston Villa, Oporto (Portugal), and Scotland before joining United in December 1972 for a reputed £15,000 a year.

LAURIE BROWN . . . "I hope it's not true."

BEFORE THE SPLIT Tommy and Agnes Docherty pictured six months ago.

The day my heart was broken and my life changed forever.

Above: The picturesque Girvan Harbour, my home town.

Below left: My wonderful mother – throughout my entire life I aspired to be half the person she was.

Below right: My first communion in March 1936.

Inset: Me aged 19, the year before Tommy trod on my toes! The stunning view behind me is what I could see from my parents' front door.

Above: My first trip south of the border – Tommy had asked me to come and look at houses in Preston and the following day we enjoyed a trip to Blackpool.

Below: The happiest day of my life – 27th December 1949.

Newlyweds! Tommy and I had only been married for three months at the time this picture was taken. I was still getting to grips with the Lancashire dialect at this point!

Happy snapshots from a happy family album.

Above left: With Michael, my eldest, in Blackpool.

Above right: Tommy and I with Catherine and Tom in the garden in Preston. A football was never far away.

Below left: Little Tom with Granny Docherty.

Below right: Catherine ready for her first day at St Monica's school in Hertfordshire.

Above: The kids enjoying a long summer day in Cockfosters.

Below: Lord of all he surveys! Tommy had just officially been appointed manager of Chelsea when this picture was taken – up until then, he had been acting manager. What would Roman Abramovich have made of this stadium?

Proudly greeting the final addition to the Docherty family. Tommy and I with Peter and, *inset*, Peter meets his brothers and sister.

Tom and Peter learning the ropes from their dad.

Above: Hand ball, ref!

Below: Me trying to understand the offside rule – although I probably understood the beautiful game a lot better than most of today's WAGs! Notice the state-of-the-art plasma TV in the background!

with his plea to watch them all over again. How I loved and still miss that boy, that young man, that innocent child in him.

At this point in our lives, he knew he had more playing days to remember than to relish and, without any qualifications, his spare time was increasingly consumed by coaching at schoolboy level. It continued to be conducted on an expenses-only basis and took him away from home for a great deal of time, but our individual roles were clearly defined. I cared for the family while he invested in our future. The odd thing was that the older he became, the better he seemed to be playing.

One specific example remains firmly fixed in my mind. Dependent on injuries or suspensions, Tommy was selected by the manager, George Swindin, at either right-half or centre-half. He preferred playing in midfield but came to realise that operating in the back four afforded him more time to 'read' the game and he honestly felt he could play in that position until he was 40. All he really required at five feet and seven inches was a taller defensive partner to take care of the occasional high and awkward cross.

By way of demonstration came the memorable afternoon of Saturday, 23 April 1960, when Arsenal beat Manchester United 5–2 at Highbury in their penultimate game of the season. The only adjective I could choose to describe his display that afternoon is majestic. I must have been right because Matt Busby made a point of visiting the home dressing room after the match to congratulate him on what he described as 'a copybook performance'.

Then Tommy went and broke his leg. And in return I received a new hairstyle from Vidal Sassoon. I'm fairly sure that it was Jimmy Greaves who first christened football 'a funny old game' and he was right. My husband fractures his leg and I get a free haircut. I remember it was towards the end of the first half against Chelsea in the middle of November 1960, as I sat next to a complete stranger whom I later discovered was apparently the talk of the nearby King's Road. The papers referred to him as the 'celebrity crimper'.

A new look was the last thing on my mind as I watched Tommy collapse in agony after a conflict of interests with his own centre-half, Bill Dodgin. They both went for the same ball (I never did understand that terminology because there only ever *is* one) in the belief they could both win it. Having discovered they were both absolutely correct, they both did. The ensuing collision saw Tommy stretchered from the field and I spent the whole of the half-time period anxiously awaiting his reappearance. When Arsenal resumed with only 10 men, as there were no substitutes permitted in those days, and I had scanned the players and quickly noticed that my husband was the predictable absentee, I immediately went to enquire about him. Bob Wall, the Arsenal secretary, informed me that Tommy had been taken by ambulance to University College Hospital for X-rays on a suspected broken leg and there would be a car waiting to transport me there from the ground at 4:30 pm in an attempt to beat the traffic at the final whistle. I had no choice other than to return to my seat.

Early in the second half, the man next to me introduced himself, told me his occupation, confessed to being an avid Chelsea supporter and asked if I was Tommy's wife. He must have known I was to have even posed the question, so when I also informed him of my husband's condition my new friend Vidal kindly asked if there was anything he could do. I politely declined – mainly because I couldn't begin to imagine how a hairdresser could possibly help in such a situation. Presumably by way of compensation, that's when he asked me if I wanted my hair done. As his guest, he insisted. We exchanged phone numbers before I left for the hospital to see how Tommy was and to tell him that Mr Sassoon had been asking after him. He was slightly befuddled from a painkilling injection and not surprisingly had never heard of the hairdresser either. Remembering the summer of 1953, I assured him that he would be fit again in no time.

The entertainers Mike and Bernie Winters arrived – quickly followed by the matron who ushered everyone out. Tommy was kept in for observation overnight and when he returned home by taxi the next morning we began to relive the regime of over seven years earlier. Of long nights and ever-larger jigsaw puzzles, passing the endless time when all he wanted was to be winning and passing the ball.

TD's progress was once again astounding but there was disappointment when he went off to have his plaster removed with his optimistically polished shoe in his hand. He returned home still holding the shoe, the doctor having told him it was too soon and to come back seven days later. What a long week that was. Eventually the cast came off and Tommy immediately launched himself into a self-devised fitness routine which culminated in a 10-mile run, whatever the weather, around the Cockfosters and Southgate district every single evening with a heavy army boot on the recuperating foot.

I was under orders to have a steaming hot bath waiting for him when he eventually arrived home. The determination and stamina of the man were phenomenal and he was back and available for selection less than three months later. Meanwhile, the stylist to the stars had been on the phone enquiring about Tommy's progress and when I would be visiting his salon. We were getting on well, me and Vidal.

Unfortunately, Tommy wasn't getting on at all well with George Swindin. The Arsenal manager had clearly been impressed by an Irish wing-half called Terry Neill, who had been deputising for Tommy. When the youngster retained his place for the North London derby against Tottenham at White Hart Lane, it was equally apparent that my fit-again husband's future in the first team looked bleak – even though Spurs won 4–2. As if to reinforce that suspicion, Mr Swindin now seemed to be scouring the game for an unsolicited future for Tommy, yet merely succeeded in delivering the ultimate insult.

From Mr Swindin's obvious scheming, Tommy was offered and declined the jobs of player-manager at first Southend and, within a fortnight, Leyton Orient. It seemed anywhere would do as far as the Arsenal hierarchy were concerned, let's just get rid of him. Then, one afternoon in early February, when Tommy had gone out for a couple of hours with the Arsenal winger Jackie Henderson, his devious boss arrived at the house. After exchanging the usual pleasantries – to be honest, I barely knew the man – he proceeded to tell me that the Blackpool manager, Ron Suart, had been in contact and Mr Swindin thought that Tommy could, as he put it to me, 'Go north and make a name for himself.'

What I politely said and what I furiously thought were very different. I told him to talk to Tommy when he came back as I never interfered with his work. What I thought was that his comments were nothing short of disgraceful.

He was actually suggesting that my husband should 'go north' to a place just down the road from Preston 'and make a name for himself'. To Lancashire, where he had performed with such distinction for nearly nine years. A county where he had played with and against the very best and had been chosen as the captain of his country. And now it was being proposed he should return there to build a career! Before hurriedly leaving – perhaps he sensed my resentment – Mr Swindin asked if I would be 'kind enough' to get Tommy to call into Highbury when he returned home.

Within minutes, the phone rang and it was Tom Finney. I told him that Tommy was out and he explained that he was calling on behalf of Ron Suart in an attempt to persuade my husband that it would be a good move for him. I hadn't seen or spoken to Tom or his wife, Elsie, since leaving Preston so we had a very pleasant conversation about our respective children and lives, but dear Tom knew just as well as I did. Come what may, Tommy would make his own decision. We said goodbye with the promises that old friends make and I passed the time until Tommy's return by picking up the phone and making an appointment for that long-standing invitation from Mr Sassoon. I loved the new shape he eventually gave my hair but now it was patently clear that we had to urgently reshape Tommy's career.

When he did get back, laughing and joking with Jackie as

usual, I stopped him in his tracks by saying, 'Well, I'll now wipe that lovely smile off your face!' He was also surprised and then perturbed that his manager had visited us. And it was about to become even more bizarre. As Tommy travelled by tube to the ground, determined now to make a name for himself in the *south*, some unknown Arsenal employee appeared with the transfer forms to Blackpool for him to sign. This was starting to look like constructive dismissal.

Tommy and I had a long discussion that night. We decided if at all possible to stay in North London, mainly as we didn't want to disrupt Michael's education. It was humiliating for my husband to discover he wasn't wanted, but help was about to arrive from that rarest of species – a trustworthy sports reporter. During our earnest conversation, Tommy said he was 'packing it in' and I told him I thought that too drastic a step. He was only 32, incredibly fit and could comfortably play for at least several more years. I considered his decision to be the knee-jerk reaction of a proud and frustrated young man but, no, he was adamant and as usual I went along with his decision.

Wouldn't you know it, he was about to retire at much the same time as the abolition of the maximum wage policy of £20 a week.

For those of you who may not know about the maximum wage policy – and how it ended – here's a brief outline. In April 1960, George Eastham, the Newcastle United winger, made the first of several unsuccessful requests to be released from his contract. The club's repeated refusal left him so frustrated and disillusioned that he actually quit the game and took a job outside football. That October, the Professional Footballers'

Association approached Eastham and asked him if he would consider becoming a test case on the questionable validity of the transfer system. With nothing to lose and at no personal expense, he agreed. The dispute centred around the right of a player to demand a transfer at the end of his contract. The PFA christened it a 'slave contract' which effectively bound its members to a club for life. Indeed, a club could retain a player's contract even if it didn't re-employ him. In January 1961, just 48 hours before threatened strike action by the players' union, the League backed down and agreed to scrap the contract system.

Newcastle had already relented and granted Eastham a transfer to Arsenal for a fee of £47,000 the previous November, but the wheels of justice had by then been set in motion and nothing in the game would ever be quite the same again. It wasn't overnight, it just seemed that way, but Johnny Haynes, the captain of Fulham and England, became the first player in this country to start earning the staggering amount of £100 a week. By then Tommy had already, as they say in the game, decided to hang up his boots.

I don't want you to think of me as subservient. I wasn't afraid to argue if I disagreed but, exactly like my dad when I was growing up, everything must have suited me or it simply wouldn't have been the way it was. I was merely trying to be realistic but I rapidly drafted Tommy's letter of retirement to Arsenal anyway. Within minutes of Tommy returning from the letterbox, James Connolly of the *Sunday Express* was on the phone. The late, much-missed Jim was a genial journalist who had his ear closer to the ground than a Basset hound out on an inquisitive evening walk. I knew he hadn't gone quite so far as to intercept the mail but it was a remarkable coincidence that he had called to tell Tommy on that of all evenings that Chelsea were looking for a first-team coach and, after their fairly lengthy chat, we quickly composed an application and off he went again to catch the last post.

It turned out to be the last post for his playing career. There was no mournful solo trumpet, but at 8:00 am the next morning a maniacal George Swindin came knocking furiously on our front door. He was waving Tommy's letter of resignation in his left hand and in my husband's face, telling him that he couldn't do such a thing. Well, he could and he already had.

Even more rewarding during this pointless tirade was the fact that Chelsea phoned to arrange an appointment later that day for their vacancy. Tommy told his imminent ex-boss that he was very sorry but would he mind leaving now as he had to start getting dressed for his interview. However, Arsenal hadn't even begun to finish. By the time they had, I seriously considered holding them in contempt of sport.

When Tommy appeared downstairs, I suggested he should go straight back up to the bedroom again. He was wearing his Arsenal blazer and I had to point out that it wasn't a very good idea to go for his interview at Chelsea in an Arsenal jacket. He went and changed into his suit, his one and only suit, and before he left I mentioned how important it was to raise the question of accommodation as we were living in a house owned by Arsenal.

I was on tenterhooks the whole time he was at Stamford Bridge and full of equal amounts of delight and despair on his eventual return. He had been instantly offered and accepted the job – but had forgotten to ask about accommodation. The following morning, as if to highlight Tommy's omission, we received a registered letter from Highbury requesting us to 'vacate the property at our earliest convenience'. I was extremely worried but Tommy casually said there was no way Arsenal would put us out on the street. However, their earlier treatment of him, coupled with the arrival of the next thinly disguised eviction notice 48 hours later, left me considerably less confident than my husband. It was a badly kept secret at the club that Arsenal had earmarked the house for George Eastham and his family.

I had to actually plead with Tommy to ask Chelsea for help. His salary when he started his new job on 10 February was still £17 a week, the only difference being a £4 win bonus and £2 for a draw. Every penny continued to be spoken for with almost every fresh postal delivery exerting more pressure from Highbury. We were living in the capital but we didn't *have* any and after several months Arsenal had naturally lost all patience.

They didn't really possess any to begin with. Tommy was so totally immersed in his new job that I realised only I could solve the problem. I didn't know where to begin until, one memorable day, I was helped by two shining knights. I had noticed a semi-detached house for sale just one street away, at 95 Belmont Avenue, Cockfosters. It had four bedrooms, was unoccupied and was on the market at £5,800 (pricey then, laughable today). Nevertheless, I made an appointment with Mr High, the manager of Barclays Bank in East Barnet. Mr High was a gem of a man who patiently assessed every single page of my carefully kept accounts. It transpired that on his 35th birthday, just two years away, Tommy was due to receive £1,000 from the Players Provident Fund, an organisation that is extinct today for obvious reasons.

Mr High told me that, if I composed a letter for Tommy to sign and send to the Football League headquarters in Lytham St Annes asking for the money to be made over to the bank when the policy matured, he could lend us the same amount with immediate effect. We required a deposit of £580 plus legal and insurance fees and, although I would later discover that the entire house needed rewiring, all we had to find now was a mortgage.

And that was where the chairman of Chelsea, Joe Mears, came riding to our rescue. He offered to give us a club loan of £5,000 at a fixed interest rate of one per cent. Imagine that – £50 annual interest on a £5,000 loan! It was the most generous gesture and one that I have never forgotten. Of course, we had to take out insurance policies to cover the loans but the sleepless nights, for me if not my professionally blinkered husband, were at last over.

Having managed to keep Arsenal at arm's length for over six months, we moved in to our new home on 23 August. Because of the various loans we'd taken out to get the house, money was tight for the next couple of years. We didn't even dare buy a daily newspaper, Tommy normally managing to pick up a discarded one at the training ground. But, after almost 12 years of marriage, we finally had our *own* home. Not only that, it came with central heating!

Within a month, there was even more good news. At least for us. Out of the Chelsea blue and after a disastrous start to the season, Ted Drake was sacked after nine years at the helm and Tommy was appointed acting manager until the end of the year. He had three months to prove himself, so, imagine our delight when, on 1 January 1962, he was officially installed as the Chelsea boss on a salary of £1,500 a year with bonuses of £6 for a win and £3 for a draw. The first call I received after this was from Vidal telling me that I 'simply must' revisit his salon for another complimentary hairstyle. At the age of 33, my husband was the manager of a First Division football club and he had virtually doubled his salary overnight. All those endless hours of schoolboy coaching coupled with his natural enthusiasm for the game were about to quite literally pay off. We weren't exactly rolling in it but I could start to see a way out of it.

Off the pitch, at least, because on it Tommy's team was caught in a downward spiral. After they were eliminated 4–3 from the FA Cup in the third round away to Second Division Liverpool, the season went from bad to worse. In fact, after beating Sheffield Wednesday 1–0 at home on 24 February, Chelsea drew five and lost six of their remaining 11 games. We were relegated – and my husband, once again without the slightest discussion, jumped on a plane bound for the capital of Spain.

CHAPTER 7

THE BLUE BOYS

Ah, but a man's reach should exceed his grasp,
Or what's a heaven for?
ROBERT BROWNING (1812–89)

Uninvited, Tommy had decided to go and observe Real Madrid, the perennial aristocrats of European football, in pre-season training for a fortnight. Somehow we managed to scrape together his £52 fare.

I think we may have sold something to friends – I do know I didn't go anywhere near a pawn shop – but the cost didn't include accommodation. He brushed that problem aside, telling me that he would introduce himself to anyone who spoke English and take it from there. It seemed to work and he came back absolutely brimming with fresh ideas and dirty laundry. At the first board meeting prior to the new campaign, Tommy informed the Chelsea directors of his unscheduled trip and the various plans and new training schedules he would like to implement as a result. The chairman happily agreed and asked about the cost of the journey. After briefly detailing his expenditure and the predictable absence of receipts, Tommy was instantly reimbursed from the secretary's petty-cash drawer. Another perfect example of the man that was Joe Mears.

In typically rollercoaster fashion, Tommy brought Chelsea straight back up the following season. For me, it evoked respectful memories of the boys who lost their lives at Munich because he was quickly (some reporters preferred the word 'ruthlessly') replacing the cynical, older players with vibrant youngsters; boys with a thirst for knowledge and success. Wages continued to be low but the collective spirit was soaring. When I took friends to a match, I could feel the wind of change and it was generally the players' parents that they met afterwards in the club lounge. Most of the boys in that team were simply too young to be married or even in a stable relationship. More than anything, that's what reminded me of the Busby Babes.

Initially, I thought I would stop going to games once Tommy finished playing, but, if anything, watching the team he managed actually made the sporting drama all the more exciting. Tommy seemed capable of imbuing his players with his own appetite for success. Whenever we scored, I would always look to where Tommy sat in the dugout far below, watching his reaction. Only at the final whistle did the tension let up, and I would stand and take huge deep breaths and finally calm down. It was simply intoxicating.

For those of you not old enough to remember, the winter of 1962 will never be forgotten. Over a six-week period, starting just before Christmas, some 400 League and Cup games were either postponed or abandoned across the country and the season was eventually extended as a result. When the snow started to incessantly fall, Chelsea were seven points clear at the top of Division Two (in the days, don't forget, of two points for a win) and promotion seemed if not a foregone conclusion then at least more likely than not. The board was obviously so pleased with Tommy's efforts that his annual salary had been increased to £2,000, a 33 per cent rise. But, as games continued to be called off, the frustrated manager received permission from Mr Mears to take the team to Malta for five days' training. When they returned and the weather finally relented, their lead was whittled away on an almost weekly basis. The snow and ice had melted and been replaced by unbridled panic.

A narrow 2–1 defeat at Old Trafford in the fifth round to eventual FA Cup winners Manchester United may have allowed the team to fully concentrate on the priority of promotion but suddenly, with two games remaining, Stoke City, Sunderland and Chelsea were now embroiled in a three-way fight for the two First Division places.

Our penultimate fixture on Saturday, 18 May 1963, was at Roker Park against Sunderland. We had to win there and then beat struggling Portsmouth at Stamford Bridge to be certain of promotion. I remember walking downstairs with a bundle of laundry just as the second-half commentary from Sunderland began on the radio. Chelsea were 1–0 ahead and I sat down on the stairs, nervously clutching my pile of washing and didn't move a muscle until the final whistle pierced the airwaves. The late Tommy Harmer scored the only goal of the game with a deflection off a delicate and unmentionable part of his anatomy! It must have brought tears to his eyes for a very different reason to my own.

Due to the backlog of postponements, the game against

Portsmouth was played the following Tuesday evening. What a night it turned out to be. We won 7–0 and, although Stoke were crowned champions by a single point, we were *up*! Tommy may have been a runner-up again but there was no heartbreak on this occasion, only elation. There was also a certain irony, because we had finished level on 52 points with Sunderland, only this time goal average had worked in our favour. When I jumped into Tommy's outstretched arms in a packed corridor after the match, he couldn't tell me how he felt as he was completely hoarse. But I knew. Of course I knew.

He had written in his programme notes one weekend towards the end of that season: 'My wife, Agnes, is the ideal wife for a football manager. She accepts that I'm dedicated to the job and knows nothing will change it. She is kept busy with the children but comes to most of our home games.' Not exactly a compliment but I never fished for those anyway.

However, I had been angling for Tommy to get some smart clothes that would suitably reflect his new-found status as a successful football manager. I still cringed at the memory of him almost going for his interview at Chelsea in an old Arsenal blazer. The problem was that Tommy possessed wide shoulders, massive thighs and very short arms and legs. In the absence of a bespoke tailor catering for the needs of a Neanderthal man, I found Peter Lelonek. He was an outfitter who, true to his job description, came to our house and fitted Tommy out. As a surprise, I asked Peter to also supply a made-to-measure Crombie overcoat. In those days, it was considered a *de rigueur* garment on touchline patrol to such an extent that no self-respecting coach would be seen without one. When

Tommy tried it on, he turned from the full-length mirror to me, smiled and said, 'I feel like I've finally arrived!'

We were definitely heading in the right direction. The previous month, Tommy's League benefit became due on his 35th birthday. We had already repaid over £600 of our three-year loan to the bank, so we settled the outstanding amount in full. Now we only had our mortgage with the club and were left with £600 in credit. We felt comparatively rich – until we were invited to the south of France and saw how the other half *really* live. Three weeks after gaining promotion, a delighted Joe Mears had transported the entire Chelsea staff, players and their wives and girlfriends to Cannes for a week. The only blot on the landscape came when Tommy and I were invited to dine with the chairman on his beautiful yacht. I felt seasick simply standing on the quay and that's precisely where I should have stayed. It may have been the gazpacho – which I had never heard of – or the steak tartare, which I *had* heard of but never tasted, or perhaps it was simply that bloody boat. Whatever it was, I have never been so violently sick in my life. Fortunately, I managed to stagger to the railings on the upper deck before emptying the contents of my stomach into the Mediterranean.

Halfway through the following season of 1963/64, Tommy received another unsolicited annual wage rise of £500, taking his salary to £2,500. Despite being knocked out of the FA Cup 2–1 at home by Second Division Huddersfield Town in the fourth round, Chelsea – with a young and inexperienced side – finished a very creditable fifth behind the champions Liverpool. And, to add to our contentment, by the end of that season I was pregnant again. I could tell many of our friends thought it was an accident, after all, our next youngest child, Tom, was almost eight, but they couldn't have been more wrong. Tommy and I had always believed in nature far more than contraception.

Just after the start of the new campaign, Chelsea were away to Aston Villa on the Monday night, 31 August (they drew 2–2). Tommy made me promise to phone him immediately if I went into labour. The baby had been due on 20 August, so I was well into extra-time when I rang Tommy on Tuesday, 1 September 1964, at 7:10 am to be met by a series of sleepy grunts. I wasn't sure exactly who was having more contractions, me or him, so I hung up and headed by taxi for the hospital. Our third son and fourth and final child, Peter, a 10 lbs 1 oz delight, was born at 10:20 am that morning. The matron had been kind enough to make a call on my behalf to the club secretary, John Battersby, so, when the team arrived back in London, Tommy was given the happy news and came straight round to see us.

I remember lying in that bed later that day with just my brand-new baby for company. I stared down at him, gently stroked his tiny, perfect features and thought, 'Life is too good to be true.' How sadly prophetic those words would eventually turn out to be.

My brothers and sisters had all by now grown up and started their own adult lives. So, it made sense for Dad to leave Preston and come and live with us. I suppose I never stopped feeling protective towards him. He thought the world of Tommy and TD was always so kind and generous to him – even to the point of allowing him to smoke in the house when he despised the habit himself. Dad was in his element with our latest addition to the family and became the perfect resident babysitter, gardener, domestic help and self-appointed librarian.

Dad would scour the daily newspapers and cut out all the articles he could find concerning his son-in-law, patiently pasting them into an ever-expanding library of thick scrapbooks. In fact, there came a time when that task alone could have become a full-time occupation. My mother-in-law also used to send us the sports pages from the Scottish editions to keep him up to date with the football scene north of the border. 'Granny's back pages' we called them.

The social life with Chelsea was becoming hectic, but Dad's constant presence enabled me to accompany Tommy to more functions than I would have otherwise been able. We mingled comfortably with celebrities from the twin worlds of sport and showbusiness. I began to realise with pride that Tommy was rapidly becoming a star himself.

Tommy was now in demand on both personal and professional levels. In fact, after a 3–0 defeat at Sunderland in the week leading up to Christmas, Tommy came home to tell me that he had been visited after the game by some Roker Park officials who enquired in whispered tones if Tommy would be interested in the manager's job up there. They were serious enough to offer him £6,000 a year before he had even boarded the team bus home. As Tommy was now earning £2,500 at Chelsea, this represented an enormous difference. We discussed it late into the night and decided that Tommy should speak to Joe Mears as soon as possible the next day.

The chairman quietly listened, thanked Tommy for his honesty regarding this illegal approach and offered him a pay rise to £4,000 with immediate effect. After the past two seasons, we had hopefully anticipated a £500 increase in salary to £3,000 so this was much better than we could have imagined. Tommy accepted of course. I didn't believe for a moment he would have walked away from Chelsea. He loved that club too much and all the hard work was starting to pay off on the pitch.

In fact, the 1964/65 season was proving to be the most successful of his admittedly brief managerial career. Yet it would also be liberally laced with disappointment and controversy before it had run its course. Chelsea were playing some breathtaking football and the team now seemed even younger than ever as Tommy continued to implement his youth policy. Then, a week before facing Liverpool in the FA Cup semi-final at Villa Park on 27 March, with the end of the season approaching, the most extraordinary thing happened.

Chelsea had reached the League Cup Final against Leicester City and, on the previous Monday, 15 March, won the first leg 3–2 at Stamford Bridge. The return leg at Filbert Street was scheduled for three weeks later, 5 April. Next up on the fixture list was a league match at home to (who else?!) Sheffield United on Saturday, 20 March. However, torrential rain throughout the week led to the match being called off. So, that Friday lunchtime, Tommy returned home and told me to pack as quickly as I could. We were going to Cannes that afternoon for five days. Just the two of us.

All this at a time when Chelsea were battling for success on all three domestic fronts. Who could have persuaded my football-obsessed husband to take a break at such a crucial point in the season? Step forward Chelsea chairman Joe Mears.

He had told Tommy he needed a break and suggested that this was the ideal time to do it. Everything had been arranged behind my back; even the kids were farmed out to various friends and neighbours without my knowledge.

We had a wonderful time in those few days alone, although reality returned with us when we lost the FA Cup semi-final 2–0 to Bill Shankly's eventual winners, Liverpool. Although we weren't to know it at the time, our dear friend Bill, the man whose mud-caked jersey had spent so many seasons at Preston running about by itself, was gradually building the foundations of the Liverpool legend.

That defeat at Villa Park gave me two sleepless nights. Not so much through bitter disappointment but because Tommy came walking into the house that evening casually carrying the FA Cup in his right hand. 'My God, what on earth are you doing with *that*?' I asked. It seemed the trophy had been on view at the match and the Football Association representative in the Midlands had asked if Chelsea could return it to their offices in London on the Monday morning. The governing body probably assumed that it would be kept safely under lock and key at Stamford Bridge. Instead, my husband had decided to bring it home.

I lay awake through both those long nights, listening to the slightest sound on the street, petrified something terrible would happen to that priceless piece of silverware. I was fairly sure that our house insurance didn't cover the theft of the FA Cup from the lounge table and thank heavens it was a year before somebody actually stole the World Cup! The children on the other hand were very excited and insisted on having numerous photographs taken with it. I even took a picture of Peter 'standing' inside it with his chubby wee hands clutching the rim. We were all naturally upset when the photos failed to come out. I hadn't checked to see if there was any film in the camera.

We drew 0–0 in the return leg of the League Cup Final with Leicester to give Tommy his first trophy as a manager and entry into the following season's Inter-Cities Fairs Cup, the curiously titled forerunner to the UEFA Cup. But now he was chasing the main prize. It was Easter and we were locked in a three-way tussle for the title with the mighty Uniteds of Leeds and Manchester.

Unfortunately for Chelsea, and in the space of seven days, the last three fixtures of the season were all away from home to Liverpool, Burnley and Blackpool. It made sense to use the seaside town as their base for the whole week and, despite losing 2–0 at Anfield on Bank Holiday Monday, 19 April, they were by no means out of contention. The last two matches were the following Saturday and Monday. But those boys in whom Tommy had placed so much trust and responsibility were about to shoot themselves in their collective feet before another ball had even been kicked.

At the pre-arranged curfew of 11:00 pm on the Wednesday, all the players had reported back to the hotel and retired to their rooms for the night. Or at least the soundly sleeping Chelsea manager thought they had until he was awakened just before 1:00 am by the night porter telling him that a fire-escape door had been left open and he suspected some of Tommy's players were missing.

A search of the rooms quickly confirmed that no fewer than eight of the squad were absent without leave. Taking a chair from the lounge, Tommy sat himself in front of the fire-escape door and waited for his errant young charges to return. It was precisely 3:46 am when the Blackpool Eight (as they were inevitably dubbed in the papers) came sneaking back in to be confronted by a ballistic boss in a fluffy white bathrobe. The guilty men were Marvin Hinton, Bert Murray, Barry Bridges, the future Chelsea managers John Hollins and Eddie McCreadie and a reserve-team player called Joe Fascione.

That's the first six. The last two deserve singling out for special attention as they went on to make major names for themselves. The first was George Graham, future Arsenal manager and renowned disciplinarian. Who knows, perhaps young George learned a valuable lesson on the rickety fire escape that night.

The last offender – and, as far as my husband was always concerned, one of the instigators – was the 22-year-old Chelsea captain, Terry Venables, later of Barcelona, Spurs and England fame. Tommy admired Terry as a player so much that he had made him the skipper at such a tender age.

Tommy would frequently return home on a Saturday night full of fatigue, complaining that Venables had once again openly questioned his tactical judgement in the pre-match or half-time team talk. He thought him a bit mouthy because it seemed that Venables would sometimes criticise him publicly in the dressing room only to apologise privately in his office later in the week. I always thought that Tommy's age didn't help. Instead of being a senior figure of authority, he could easily have passed for most of that team's elder brother.

Anyway, the miscreants had apparently slipped out to a local bowling alley called the Savoy Bowl and, according to members of staff there who were later interviewed by reporters, none of them had all that much to drink. It seemed the local girls were far more intoxicating. However, Tommy didn't know this at the time.

Having had the best part of four hours to consider what punishment to hand out, Tommy's decision was controversial, to say the least. Instead of a fine or a good old-fashioned dressing down, Tommy went a lot further. When he called me at 7:00 am and explained the situation, I could tell from his voice that he hadn't slept for the rest of the night, but also that his mind was firmly made up – even if his decision would ultimately cost Chelsea any chance of the championship.

As the squad shuffled silently into the dining room half an hour later, the eight sets of bleary eyes were stunned to find the return portion of their train tickets to London lying on their cold and otherwise empty breakfast plates. Tommy was sending them all home.

Naturally, the news caused a sensation, but my husband was totally unrepentant. Part of his statement read: 'I know I have deliberately prejudiced our chances of winning the League Championship because I believe in sticking to a principle. Discipline is more important than any honour in football.'

Nor was I surprised to read the accompanying quote from Joe Mears: 'I am sure Tommy has done the right thing and will have the fullest support of the club board.'

Saturday, 24 April, was Tommy's 37th birthday. His present that day was a scoreline of Burnley 6 Chelsea 2. The team's title hopes were in tatters but I knew he bore neither regrets nor grudges. Indeed, seven of the eight 10-pin bowlers (apart from the reserve, Fascione) were recalled for the final game at Blackpool, which they lost 3–2, and no further action was taken against them. Manchester United won the title and Leeds finished as runners-up on goal average. If Tommy was depressed or ever privately questioned his decision to send those players packing, he certainly never showed it to me. In fact, less than a week after the season finished, he came bounding through the door and said, 'Come on, we're going to Paris for the weekend.'

He had been to that most beautiful of cities several times for pre-season friendlies but never before as a tourist. It was like a second honeymoon as we dined near the top of the Eiffel Tower, strolled and laughed hand-in-hand along the Champs Elysees and generally behaved the way that young lovers do in Paris in the springtime.

Chelsea completed the following season of 1965/66 once again empty-handed but it was still another successful campaign. Think about it for a moment. Tommy had virtually – some might say recklessly – ripped up the rulebook and started from scratch. He had been the manager of a top First Division team for over four years, was now earning £4,500 a year before bonuses and yet, at the age of 38, he was still younger than some players plying their trade in the Premier League today. With the almost unconditional and fatherly support of his chairman, Tommy had set the blue touch paper of youth alight and retired to witness the outcome. For such a young team, the results were appropriately explosive.

They finished fifth in the League (10 points behind the champions, Shankly's Liverpool), were losing FA Cup semi-finalists again (this time 2–0 to Sheffield Wednesday) and also reached the semi-finals of the Fairs Cup. They lost 2–0 away to Barcelona in the first leg but managed to beat the Spanish giants by the same scoreline in the return fixture. The toss of a coin determined that a third play-off match on 25 May would be staged in the Catalan capital. I was among the crowd at Stamford Bridge who watched what would be our final game of that season on a giant screen erected on the pitch. It was men against boys and we lost 5–0, but even I could tell that those youngsters had learned lessons that can't be taught on the training ground.

Tommy was in the process of blending the agility of Peter Bonetti in goal with the destructiveness of Ron 'Chopper' Harris in defence, the industry of John Hollins in midfield and the craft of Charlie Cooke on the wing to the raw genius of a teenage striker called Peter Osgood. Ask any Chelsea supporter of a certain age to name their favourite team and I promise you that particular one will feature high on their list. Yet, like so many things in my husband's life, it became a question of what might have been; of unfulfilled promise. At least Matt Busby could spend the rest of his days pointing to the act of an unkind God followed by eventual fulfilment. Tommy can only stare into the bathroom mirror and silently wonder.

Mr Mears once again showed his appreciation by treating the entire squad to 10 days on the Cote d'Azur. I was unable to make the trip as two of the children were suffering from post-vaccination fever. Four days before they were due to leave for Cannes, I received an anonymous letter telling me that my husband was having an affair with the wife of one of his young players.

It was such a ludicrous accusation that I didn't even bother to show it to Tommy. Instead, I just laughed and tore it up, safe in the knowledge that he wouldn't dream of doing that to me.

CHAPTER 8

BETRAYAL

Several excuses are always less convincing than one.
ALDOUS HUXLEY (1894–1963)

Her name was Maria and she wasn't the wife of a Chelsea player at all. She *was* married but she was also German and lived in Munich. That's as much as I will say about her identity, as she had at the time a nine-year-old daughter whom I have no wish to embarrass with her mother's infidelity. That wee girl is a middle-aged woman now and perhaps has children of her own.

But of all the places in the world. Munich. The city where a dream had died on a stretch of tarmac some eight years earlier. And of all the names in the world. Maria. The heroine in one of my favourite films, *West Side Story*. Remember the romantic lyric sung by Richard Beymer as Tony about his ill-fated lover, played by Natalie Wood? 'Maria! I just met a girl named Maria/and suddenly that name/will never be the same to me.' Well, it never meant quite the same to me either.

Like the pioneering Busby before him, my husband had always been a firm believer in the benefits of regular European competition. It presented an opportunity to learn from and test yourself against foreign opposition, so I thought no more of it when, just three days after returning from France, Tommy told me that he was going to Germany on 6 June to spend a week studying Bayern Munich's training methods. I wondered why Bayern would be training at that time of the year at all but put it down to the typical professionalism of that country. Upon his return, Tommy casually mentioned that he had met a nice family who had provided him with free meals and accommodation and, to reciprocate, he had invited them to stay with us in London for a holiday. Not only that, but they would be arriving within 48 hours and staying for 10 days.

I had learned long ago to accept such largesse and lack of notice from Tommy. Similarly, I thought it mere coincidence when he subsequently arranged for Chelsea to play a series of pre-season friendlies against Stuttgart, Hamburg and Eintracht Frankfurt in Germany later that summer. However, I did find it slightly strange when he proudly announced that he had also started learning the language.

With Tommy's new German friends arriving any day now, Dad was sent off to stay with my brother John in Preston. But, with four children of our own, we still had a problem finding places for everyone to sleep. In the end, Tommy and I surrendered our bedroom and took Dad's room, while the kids squeezed in with each other. In the meantime, Tommy drove down to one of the ports to pick up Maria, her husband and their daughter.

Maria and her family spoke no English, so communication was a problem. Fortunately, we had some good friends, Ron Goodman and his wife, Christiana, living nearby. Christiana was German, so she and Ron came over for dinner nearly every night of the visit and Christiana acted as a tireless translator. During the day, Tommy conducted sightseeing tours – something we had rarely done with our own children since arriving in London – and we all went swimming and for long walks in the nearby forest.

Then the strangest thing occurred. On their penultimate night, we were invited over to Ron and Christiana's for dinner. As we left after the meal, Tommy asked me to drive and jumped into the back seat of the car alongside Maria. That was unusual in itself, as Tommy never particularly liked being a passenger, but, as I looked over my shoulder to reverse on to the main road, I saw them holding hands. This German woman and my husband, holding hands as if it were the most natural thing in the world. Call me naïve, but at the time all I thought was, 'That's funny', and left it at that.

Then, waiting silently at a set of red traffic lights on our way to a West End restaurant on their last evening as our guests and with Tommy back behind the wheel, Maria suddenly burst into tears. I turned around in concern and listened in ignorance as she and her husband had what appeared to be quite an earnest discussion. With Tommy's rudimentary help, they managed to establish the fact that it was actually nothing. There was no cause for alarm – his wife was simply tired. I knew how she felt. It had been a long and exhausting visit and I for one was glad it was over.

I felt as though I now needed a holiday, a place to unwind – and take time to rewind the images that were by now constantly playing through my mind. We had booked a fortnight in Magaluf, Majorca, towards the end of June as the World Cup was due to start on 11 July and Tommy had been contracted to work as a summariser for the BBC. We were only taking Michael and Peter, as Catherine and Tom were still involved in school exams. Dad had been recalled from his enforced holiday so I knew they would be in safe hands. I only wished the same could have been said for my future.

The holiday proceeded pleasantly until Friday, 1 July. Michael was almost 14 years older than our youngest child, but it was wonderful to watch the enjoyment he derived from playing with his wee brother and Peter in turn absolutely worshipped Michael. At the start of that second week, Tommy had gone into Palma for the morning, ostensibly to shop. Only later did I consider the probability that it was to make a long-distance call to some suburb of Munich.

With Tommy away, I watched Michael and his little brother play football on the beach – and then sat intrigued as they were joined by an extremely good-looking young man. With his tanned skin and jet-black hair he looked like a local, but still he seemed vaguely familiar to me. Eventually, all three of them breathlessly arrived on the veranda. With a giggling Peter draped upside down over his left shoulder and having obviously been told our surname by Michael, he extended his right hand and politely introduced himself in the broadest of Belfast accents. 'Hello, Mrs Docherty,' he said. 'It's a pleasure to meet you. My name's George Best.'

In the years that would unfold and as I read the frequent, often lurid headlines, I would sometimes wonder how many destructive and alcohol-fuelled 'happy hours' that tortured young man must have spent with pathetic hangers-on in so many bars around the world before his untimely death and if he remembered those innocent couple of hours that he enjoyed with my sons. He even joined us for an orange juice and the only hard thing in his glass was the ice.

We weren't to know it, but our paths would cross again some seven years later when an older but none-the-wiser George would blame Tommy for the collapse of his career at Manchester United. That was one of Best's many problems. He could always find somebody else to blame for his own inadequacies. Perhaps he and my husband had more in common than either of them realised.

Except for one essential difference. George was a genius who happened to have been born without a brain. How many young men in this world would have done a deal with the Devil to be blessed with the God-given ability that boy possessed? Somebody should have charged him long ago with the wilful destruction of talent.

It was early afternoon by the time we said our goodbyes to one of the greatest players to ever – albeit fleetingly – grace the game. Tommy still hadn't arrived but the hotel receptionist informed me that a telegram had. Telegrams rarely bring good news and this was no exception. When I looked at the message, it informed me that Joe Mears was dead. That delightful man, who had planted Tommy's foot on the bottom rung of both the managerial and property ladders, had been enjoying a stroll through a park in Oslo on his summer holiday when he collapsed and died instantly. The death of the Chelsea chairman signalled the beginning of the end to Tommy's reign as the manager of that club.

I told Tommy the sad news when he finally did return and he immediately made arrangements to return to London, insisting that I and the boys stay behind. Knowing my husband as I believe I once did, I think he couldn't begin to contemplate lounging in the Spanish sunshine when the person who had become a father figure to him was lying on a cold slab in a mortuary.

Twenty years later, Tommy was quoted as saying that, if Joe Mears had lived, he would still have been the manager of Chelsea. It's true. They had a mutual respect and fondness for one another and, more importantly, Joe, whose father had founded the club in 1905, had a gentle way of containing Tommy's more expansive and consequently expensive ideas. The last of Joe's many considerate acts to Tommy had been to award him a new, again unsolicited, and improved five-year contract on a salary of £5,500 a year to take effect from 1 January 1967. With that in mind, we had decided to move closer to Stamford Bridge.

We moved into 4 Beltane Drive, Wimbledon, on 7 September 1966. It cost £17,250 and was a lovely house. It was so close to the All England Lawn Tennis Club that, during Wimbledon fortnight, it was possible to hear the umpire and applause drifting on the gentle breeze from the famous Centre Court. But we would only hear the muffled strains of '30–40' for one summer. Now the Chelsea chairman was gone our time at the club was almost up as well. In addition, I was about to embark on a period of my life that, in the same way as almost a decade later, I genuinely cannot believe I survived either mentally or physically.

My enduring nightmare began on 13 October that year. I had travelled back to Preston at the start of the week to helplessly watch as Graeme died on that day from cancer. He was my little sister Margaret's son and he was beautiful. He was also just 22 months old. There are no appropriate words to describe that dreadful time so forgive me if I don't even try.

It was so personal, so traumatic that I even hesitate to mention it. I hope Margaret will forgive me for recalling those dark days but I feel it's necessary to illustrate my torment. All I know is that I never forgave the man upstairs for his unnecessary cruelty towards wee Graeme and his family any more than Matt and Jean Busby probably ever could for the tragic events of Munich. But I think that was the day when my previously unswerving faith first began to waver.

Within three weeks of going home, I started to suffer severe pain up the back of my neck and head. Initially, I thought it may somehow be connected with the ordeal of seeing my nephew lose his weak fight for life and I tried desperately to ignore it because there was always too much to do. But, when the discomfort started to constantly keep me awake at night, Tommy arranged an appointment through the club doctor with an orthopaedic specialist.

After X-rays, studies of my medical history and various consultations, it seemed that my stupid leap of faith in the larder almost 14 years earlier that resulted in a miscarriage had come back to further haunt me. As if the original outcome hadn't caused enough suffering.

Sitting alongside my husband, I was informed that the force of the impact had caused the fifth and sixth vertebrae on my spine to cross, rupturing a disc and causing an abnormal bone growth to form. The doctors were astonished that I had suffered little or no reaction in the ensuing years, let alone also given birth to three more children. Apparently as a result, there was severe muscle wastage in my upper arms and they placed me in a lightweight cervical collar for several months prior to an operation, telling me that I had two choices. Major surgery or eventually becoming wheelchair-bound for the rest of my life. No choice at all, really.

The medical term for this most delicate of operations, I discovered, is Anterior Cervical Discectomy and Fusion. In their language, the surgeon makes a long, horizontal incision in your neck and separates the soft tissue before the herniated disc irritating the nerve is removed. After enlarging the space between the vertebrae above and below the removed disc, the doctor then 'plugs' the opening with a wedge-shaped bone graft, obtained from your hip through a second incision. In the healing process, the graft and vertebrae hopefully grow together.

Blinded by both science and the winter sunshine, we left my surgeon Mr Bonney's rooms in Harley Street and had been walking for an awfully long time when I realised that Tommy was almost in a trance. I asked him where he had parked and he admitted that he couldn't remember. He was lost in his own thoughts and now we had also misplaced the car. I have never possessed any sense of direction and it was over an hour before we were reunited with our vehicle.

I was generally able to return to normality – except that our lives were no longer normal. Tommy was making monthly trips to Germany on a Sunday morning and returning late on the Tuesday night. He had always admired their professionalism and almost methodical approach to sport and, although we hadn't discussed it, I had a sneaking suspicion that Tommy eventually hoped to work over there. I had bought him a set of Linguaphone records and he was progressing so well that I also decided to learn the language.

Our earlier fears that the death of Joe Mears would signal the beginning of the end of our time at Chelsea were proving to be well-founded. Joe had been replaced as chairman by Charles Pratt and TD seemed constantly on edge. He came home from a board meeting one afternoon to exclaim, 'The main problem is there are too many chiefs and not enough Indians!'

I knew his days there were numbered and increasingly I was beginning to wonder if our own were as well because, regardless of his insistence that the visits to Munich were strictly related to football, I had started to strongly suspect they were mainly to do with Maria.

Tommy would be predictably offhand on his return – irrational behaviour that I would recognise again over a decade later – and I began to resent the frequency of those trips so much that, when he told me of his next planned journey, I suggested he should take Catherine with him, that the experience would be good for her. He wasn't keen (neither was my daughter) but for once I put my foot down and she accompanied her father.

I vividly remember the date that I woke up – perhaps in

more ways than one – and realised I couldn't continue living my life like this any more. It was the morning of Thursday, 8 December, when I sat in the kitchen and asked my husband if he was having an affair with Maria. He became very angry and vehemently denied it. I suppose I should have told him that I had seen them holding hands in the back of our car but he probably would have claimed that he was only being friendly and warming them up for her. On a lovely summer's evening.

For many years, in fact since Michael's birth, I had developed several lumps in both of my upper and lower arms. Naturally, I had consulted my doctor about them but he told me they were nothing to worry about. Each roughly the size of half a hard-boiled egg, they were more unsightly than painful but, at the turn of the year, the consultant decided that one should be randomly removed for examination prior to my spinal operation.

Tommy dropped me off for my overnight stay at St Stephen's Hospital in Fulham on his way into work. When he came back at visiting time that afternoon, there was something about his entire demeanour that frightened me. I knew that man better than he knew himself, or at least I thought I did at that time, so I could instantly sense his unease and realised the moment of truth had arrived with him.

Grateful to have a private room at such a moment, I told him that *this* time he had better tell me what was wrong. I watched him sit down, clutching the unwanted grapes and box of chocolates and, before he had a chance to reply, I said, 'It *is* another woman, isn't it?'

He cleared his throat and whispered, as if we were in a public ward, 'Yes.'

At last, a confession.

'And,' I continued, 'it *is* Maria, isn't it?' I already knew the answer and all he could do was avoid my stare and slowly nod his head.

It seemed too obvious at that moment. How could I have been so foolish? But this overlooks one very important point: I just didn't believe that Tommy could have let me down so badly. I actually remember asking him how far it had gone! He was the be-all and end-all of my world and, after his career, I thought I meant the same to him. He had always told me, convinced me, that I was so very special to him.

This took place on Wednesday, 4 January 1967. Donald Campbell had lost his life on Coniston Water in the Lake District that morning, attempting the world water speed record in his jet-powered *Bluebird*. Through my tears of despair in a lonely hospital bed that night, I once again tried to apply a sense of perspective. A man had died in the pursuit of his dream of achieving 300 miles an hour– and I was living a nightmare in slow motion.

I had loved my husband so much, been so proud of him, never thought to question him until the moment I finally realised that it was during a part of that European adventure the previous season, when Chelsea drew 2–2 away to TSV Munchen in the first leg of their Fairs Cup quarter-final on 15 March 1966, that Tommy may first have met Maria.

When I arrived home from hospital, relieved to have been told that the lumps in my arms were apparently benign, nothing more was said on the subject of Maria. What more was there to say? I occupied our bedroom and he silently accepted the fact that he would now be sleeping in the newly created guest room for the foreseeable future – assuming we had one.

My children were very, *very* important to me but Tommy had been my *life* and now he didn't want to know me. Or I him, for that matter. I reassured myself that, if the children happened to notice the new sleeping arrangements and were at all puzzled, I would tell them that as a result of my spinal collar I required total isolation to avoid the possibility of accidental injury during the night. Fortunately, due to the discomfort, I had already been told that I was allowed to take it off when I went to bed but what I couldn't remove were the constant feelings of anger and betrayal. Time seemed to increase the anguish rather than assuage it and, if I had to say exactly how long we lived those separate lives, I would only be guessing. There was no point in counting the days because I hadn't set myself any sort of deadline. I wasn't an innocent prisoner chalking off time on a wall, although I often felt as if I was being unfairly punished. Nor did I feel that I could confide in anybody. After my mum's death, if I ever had a problem other than financial throughout my early adult life, I would always turn to Tommy for comfort or advice. Now, *he* was the problem.

I warned him one night in a rare conversation during our lengthy standoff that, if he ever went back to Germany, once more, just once, I would leave him. I was bluffing, of course, but he wasn't to know that. Nor could he have imagined how determined I was to prevent Maria from totally wrecking everything that I held so dear to my heart.

As the days slowly turned into weeks, I lay alone in the middle of the night and made a mental list of the respective merits of separation or reconciliation. I didn't know if telling him to leave would end my misery or merely compound it. So, if there was no game for him to attend, we would eat and pretend to play happy families with the children and, after I had put them to bed, we would sit in the silence of our small lounge and watch television together before one or other of us mumbled a meaningless goodnight. I didn't want to deprive my children of their father, even if he was barely there, any more than I wanted to lose my husband because I still loved him. My quandary was that I didn't know if I was prepared to ever forgive him.

Several very tense weeks later, Tommy came home to inform me that he was arranging to bring Maria and her daughter over to England and he was going to find somewhere for them to live. With him.

My response was immediate: 'Over my dead body!' I accompanied this with a smack across the face. It sounded like a branch snapping underfoot and I could scarcely believe I had done it. Tommy, the child in him coming to the fore, ran straight upstairs to his room – before I even had the chance to send him there.

Then, as I tossed and turned my way through the nights that followed, tearfully wondering what was happening to us, I would often hear him getting up at 3:00 or 4:00 am. He would drive away and I wouldn't see him again until dinnertime that evening. It was futile trying to talk to him, so I could only presume from his nocturnal activities that Maria had come over to England for a holiday. Or perhaps permanently.

But, almost stubbornly, I continued to strive for some semblance of normality. I had decided that I had absolutely no intention of allowing my husband to destroy everything we had worked so hard for together. His burgeoning career, his reputation, our marriage, our children, our home. Our lives.

I knew my own life was coming apart at the seams but I went to every Chelsea home game and behaved as though everything was absolutely fine. However, my weight had plummeted from a healthy 9 stones 6 lbs to a skeletal 7 stones 10 lbs. I told anyone who asked it was due to the worry of my impending operation.

Somewhere in the mist of those missing months, I came round in the middle of the night to find my dad at the foot of the bed, gently putting a pair of his socks on my feet. I turned the bedside lamp on and asked him what on earth he was doing in my room. He sat down with a resigned expression and explained that a light had woken him up. He had walked downstairs and found me curled up in a corner of the living room, crying and apparently mumbling, 'It'll be all right, Mum, won't it? *Please* tell me it'll be all right.'

She had been dead for more than 12 years and her loving, widowed husband had carried his 38-year-old wee girl back upstairs, fetched some tea and a hot water bottle and was simply trying to get her warm. The next morning, naturally and painfully aware of the situation, my dad sat uncomfortably alongside me over a cup of tea (mine) and a cigarette (his) and summoned up the courage that I could almost see him searching to find. Eventually, he said, 'Look, hen, Tommy is only a man. If women make it easy for him then, well, it must be very difficult.'

I replied, 'Well, I'm only a woman but I would never let *him* down like that.'

Michael left school that April to do all he had ever wanted to do since he had been old enough to walk and that was to play professional football. With my own memories of being forcibly removed from school, I tried to persuade him to continue his education and then pursue a career in the game but I was wasting my breath and predictably received no support from Tommy in the matter. Fortunately, it appeared that my eldest son had a reasonable chance of making the grade, because West Ham and Queens Park Rangers both wanted him to sign for them on a trial basis. And even I became excited when Bill Shankly phoned our house to ask if my son would consider signing for Liverpool.

But Tommy was determined that he should go to Burnley. In those days, that friendly club so close to Preston had an envious conveyor belt of talent coming through the ranks and TD, aware of the burden of expectation that our surname now carried, believed that Michael would get a better, fairer opportunity there. He called the manager, Harry Potts, to see if he was interested and the Burnley manager was delighted.

On the other hand, I was very sad the morning I went upstairs to help my eldest son pack for his new life in Lancashire. I could only assume he was too when I found him sitting on his bed in tears. I was wrong. His father had just told him about his affair with Maria. Michael was just 16 and a fine young man. He was kind, helpful, courteous and I loved him so much. But he was innocent and quite naïve in some ways while I was simply livid. How dare Tommy upset my son as he was about to leave home and live in digs at such a tender age? It was unforgivable. I hugged my sobbing boy for several minutes before storming downstairs to find the object of my rage standing nervously in the kitchen. And, for the second time in my life, I slapped his face.

It felt immensely satisfying and I was almost starting to get a taste for it. My only regret was that Catherine saw me do it, as I never liked to involve the children in domestic disputes. That was also unforgivable on my part. Michael's father was driving him to Burnley and, after cheerfully waving my eldest son off on his new adventure, I went inside and wept for over an hour. I have always cried in private.

Even now, all these years later, I find this part of my life almost too distressing to write down. January had been slowly followed by February, March and into early April. Nothing new in that order – except that my life no longer had any order to it. The days, the weeks, the months had lost all relevance. I can only estimate that it was around Easter time when Ronnie Corbett, the diminutive comedian and a good but unsuspecting friend, treated us to dinner at the popular Nick's Diner in Ifield Road, near Chelsea's ground. Not surprisingly, it was owned by someone called Nick and he had recently opened another place opposite. It was called The Place Opposite. I don't recall his surname but Nick obviously didn't waste too much time deliberating over names for his establishments.

I still had no specific date for my operation other then 'imminent', so I allowed Tommy to take me to the new restaurant later that month and we both tried very hard to be as we had once so effortlessly been. Perhaps too hard. I remember thinking to myself, 'What's the point if you have to try?' At one stage in our stilted conversation, I once again asked TD to swear to me that he would never return to Germany to see Maria. I knew it was inevitable that he would have to revisit that country at some stage or another in the course of his career. I just needed to know that it wouldn't involve her.

He promised – before adding that he would 'like to go back just one more time, to see how she's getting on now'. I asked him what he meant by that and he slowly stared down at his sirloin steak before replying, 'She was pregnant but she isn't any more. She hasn't slept with her husband for over a year, so I know that it was our baby. I just want to make sure she's all right. Surely you can understand that?'

I don't think I made a sound – other than dropping my knife and fork as if they were about to scald me. I do remember running out of the restaurant without collecting my coat from the cloakroom, hailing a black cab and crying all the way home.

My dad answered the door as I blindly fumbled in my handbag for the keys and, without a word, I ran straight past him to the bathroom upstairs. I was violently sick and then, as I ran the cold water tap and stared back at my tear-stained face and smudged mascara in the mirror, I kept telling myself, 'That's it, that's the end.'

My marriage was over and I wouldn't fight any more to keep him. I vowed that Tommy Docherty could go and destroy himself – but I would be damned if I let him take me or my children with him.

CHAPTER 9

THE END OF
THE AFFAIR

Then, must you speak
Of one that loved not wisely but too well.

WILLIAM SHAKESPEARE (1564–1616)

Apart from my children, life seemed pointless. One dreary day was followed by another weary night and I didn't want to be in the same room or even the same house as the man I had once worshipped.

That's why I decided to drive up to Preston with Peter for a few days and stay with my brother, John. I also wanted to spend some time with Margaret and see how she was coping after losing her baby son, Graeme, in such tragic circumstances. On top of that, I was becoming increasingly concerned about the complexity of my impending operation and realised without wishing to sound too melodramatic that I could end up in a wheelchair for the rest of my life.

So, as I slowly packed a suitcase in 'my' bedroom, Tommy appeared at the door, saw what I was doing and immediately broke down in tears. I had only ever seen the Munich disaster reduce him to such a level of raw emotion before. He begged me not to leave him and I promised him I was only going to see John and Margaret. I don't think he believed me because he tried to hold me, tried to tell me how much he loved me, how special I was, how sorry he was to have hurt me as he had done, that it would *never* happen again.

Then he dropped to his knees and once again I was staring down at a wee boy who wanted all the bad things to go away. The things he had so callously created. We rarely talked any more but I do recall once asking him, 'What if it had been me – if I'd been the one that had the affair?' He had instantly replied, 'You would have been out of that door so fast your feet wouldn't have touched the floor.' At least I knew that was honest. I changed my mind about travelling north that afternoon, which was just as well. Suddenly, Tommy would not let me out of his sight. It was quite clear to me from that moment that the affair with Maria had ended. To this day, I don't know how or why. I never asked whether the loss of her baby was the direct result of a miscarriage or an abortion. I've always felt that sometimes in life it's best not to know all the details.

It was typical of the man that he decided to court me all over again without for a moment grasping the enormity of the task. I had built an emotional wall of protection and it was so high that I doubted he would ever be capable of scaling it. I was, I thought, justifiably stubborn. An ungrateful recipient of a constant stream of presents, flowers and chocolates. He went to work and came straight home.

There were regular phone calls when he was away and he

even accompanied me to the ballet and opera – although I do recall digging him in the ribcage on one occasion when his snoring threatened to drown out the entire violin section at the Royal Albert Hall. My grovelling husband – for that is what he had become – made a tremendous effort to renew my faith in him, my love for him, but it was many more months before we shared our lives to the full again. I had lived a nightmare and in his own but very different way I think he had, too.

In time, we were unbelievably happy and I trusted him and his word to never put us through such an experience again. In retrospect, I don't think it's particularly a weakness but maybe some people only believe what they want to believe. And perhaps, certainly where my husband was concerned, I was one of those people.

Chelsea finished ninth that season to the champions Manchester United, but, after three FA Cup semi-finals in succession, we had finally made it to Wembley by beating Leeds United 1–0 with a header from Tony Hateley. The opponents on Saturday, 20 May 1967, would be our London rivals, Tottenham Hotspur. Little did I know that I would be nowhere near the grand old stadium that afternoon. Towards the end of April, the pain in my neck, back and arms had become so excruciating that I sometimes wondered if my weekly physiotherapy sessions were actually creating more of a problem than being part of the solution.

Although Tommy continued to give me much more of his time than he had ever done in all our years together, I was only too aware of the various commitments of the manager of a team about to play in the FA Cup Final. So I said nothing and made an appointment with Mr Bonney. He immediately sent me to the X-ray department and, having looked at the results, told me that surgery was necessary. Now. He wanted me admitted to hospital on Friday, 12 May, for the operation to take place four days later. I apologised and told him it was not possible as Chelsea were in the Cup Final the following Saturday. Mr Bonney was having none of it. He explained to me in layman's terms the repercussions of not having the operation. He asked me to picture a crumbling concrete pillar and compare it to the column that supported my back. He stressed that the excitement of jumping up and down at a football match could easily cause the pillar to collapse, crippling me for life.

I went home in both a taxi and a daze before telling Dad. He listened intently, then said, 'There'll be other Cup Finals, love. Go and get the job done.'

Tommy and I were still tentatively rebuilding our relationship and I hesitated about telling him for nearly a week. When I did, he told me that we had no other choice, I must do as the consultant had advised. Our friends, the Goodmans, kindly offered to look after Peter and I arranged through an agency to hire a housekeeper for two months. I was frightened, dreadfully underweight and not feeling too well, but Mr Bonney was nothing if not insistent. He was also a genius.

That man basically slit my throat from just below one ear to the other, delicately moved my larynx to one side and then spent the next seven and a half hours removing the overhanging piece of bone that was threatening the spinal column, before fusing the two offending vertebrae together with a bone graft from my right hip.

Every time I felt myself coming round after the operation, a needle appeared from nowhere to put me out again. I vaguely remember the silhouette of an evening suit – I discovered much later that Tommy was inside it – and an unfamiliar voice saying, 'She's had five pints.' I thought they were talking about my order with the milkman rather than the transfusion and remember saying to myself, 'But I usually only get four.'

I regained full consciousness on the Thursday morning and instantly wished I hadn't. The pain was unbelievable. I saw the nurse sitting at the desk with her back to me and tried to speak but nothing happened. I later learned that I had over 30 stitches along my throat and bandages up to my chin. I was also very scared, feeling as if I was slowly choking and unable to alert anybody.

The Cup Final itself was a bit of a blur. I know I watched in hospital with my neighbours and dear friends, Joan Clarke and Pam Miller, but my only certain recollection of that day is that our young side seemed to freeze due to the enormity of the occasion and we lost 2–1.

One way and another, it had been quite a traumatic week. I received flowers, cards, chocolates I couldn't eat and several bottles of champagne I couldn't drink from friends and Chelsea supporters alike. Tommy came straight from the post-match dinner and I suspect the sight of me prevented him from feeling too full of self-pity about the outcome of the game.

The stitches were removed in batches over a three-day period and I was measured for a plaster cast harness and collar which fastened under the arms and across the neck. I was sent to a nursing home in Eastbourne for a fortnight to recuperate and, upon my return, I had intended to remove the device before Christiana brought Peter home. But he came dashing in to see me before I had the chance to do so, took one look and cowered into the corner. My wee boy was staring at a skeletal, virtual stranger wearing some sort of monstrous contraption. But there's nothing as adaptable as small children. Within days of becoming accustomed to my appearance, he was desperate to try it on himself, convinced it would transform him into some kind of superhero from his favourite comic book.

I was delighted to see my own little gang again and everybody practically fell over themselves to be helpful. My lack of mobility made the children more aware of the household chores than ever before and I think the experience was good for them. But by then I strongly suspected they were also desperate to see the back of the hired housekeeper. When she had finally left to the sound of barely stifled cheers, I remember starting to wash up once only to discover that the collar prevented me from being able to look down into the sink. Tommy continued to be his new, supportive self and not only rented a new invention called a colour television but also bought me a portable black and white one for the bedroom.

But I hated feeling so weak and helpless and it came as a great relief when the cast was finally removed at the beginning of October. It had been almost five months and literally a millstone around my neck. Now I could mow the lawn, I could drive, I could even wash up. I felt really well, strong and, most importantly of all, happy. But I would never wish to relive 1967 again. I had finished with that year, apart from one problem – that year had far from finished with me. In fact, by the end of it and not for the first time in my unpredictable life with Tommy, I would be living somewhere I wouldn't even have been able to show you on the map.

I suppose I should have listened to the national news on the morning of Friday, 6 October, because, when Tommy phoned me from Stamford Bridge at about 11:30 am and asked me to call a taxi and meet him at a little Italian restaurant on the Fulham Road that we had always liked, *Trattoria Positano*, I should have known that he wasn't thinking of treating me to an early lunch. I wasn't even curious when he mentioned I should bring some writing paper and an envelope with me. But when we had been shown to our usual table in a discreet corner and he calmly explained that he wanted me to draft his resignation letter to Chelsea for him, I half-jokingly asked him if there was something I may have missed. He sighed and said, 'Bermuda, love. You missed Bermuda.'

I stared at him in bemusement for a moment before replying, 'What are you talking about?'

Naturally, I recalled that part of Chelsea's pre-season tour in early June when I was recovering from my operation had been to the island of Bermuda but only now did Tommy explain that he had been involved in 'a stupid argument' with a local referee during one of their games. It seemed that the Football Association considered the matter to be a serious one. The match official was black and part of Tommy's outburst could easily have been construed as racist, though Tommy was in no way racist. No one said it outright, but it was written between the lines of every newspaper I would later read.

Tommy had been charged with misconduct and, that

morning before he phoned me, a three-man independent commission at the Queen's Hotel in Leeds had fined him £100 and, far more importantly, suspended him from world football for 28 days with effect from Monday, 19 October. He was effectively banned from entering any ground in this country or abroad – even as a paying spectator. It meant he couldn't watch a game on a nearby playing field if that particular club was either affiliated to the FA or the world governing body of FIFA. He wasn't even allowed to watch his 11-year-old son play for his school. The Chelsea striker Tony Hateley was fined £50, severely censured and warned as to his future conduct.

I couldn't believe Tommy's ban was the result of no more than a minor altercation between a manager and a match official in a meaningless pre-season friendly. My suspicions regarding the racial undertones were confirmed by the mass coverage that accompanied the subsequent story of Tommy's resignation. Front-page headlines such as: DOC RESIGNS AS CHELSEA BOSS were followed lower down the broadsheets by: 'So what exactly did happen in Bermuda?'

Well, this is what apparently happened – and it was clearly far more serious than Tommy had intimated over our impromptu lunch. In a game played in torrential rain against a Bermudan FA representative team on 10 June, the late Chelsea winger Peter Houseman had attempted to pass to Hateley but the ball ran harmlessly out of play. Hateley swore in frustration at his team-mate and was immediately sent off for using foul and abusive language. Tommy ran on to the pitch shouting to his captain, Eddie McCreadie: 'That's it, Eddie. Bring them all off!' The watching secretary of the local FA, Joseph Ferreira, scurried down from the main stand in an attempt to defuse the situation but Tommy had turned on him and, expletives deleted, screamed, 'A referee like that shouldn't be allowed loose on a pitch! He should be locked up in a cage!'

Mr Ferreira replied, 'You may do things like this in England but you cannot do this sort of thing out here.'

Tommy evidently yelled back, 'We don't have lunatics like him in England!'

Later, the secretary told reporters, 'I had no alternative but to report all this to the Football Association. Mr Docherty's actions here were absolutely degrading. He used disgusting language.'

By the time the Chelsea chairman, Mr Pratt, had called the Italian restaurant four months later, it was shortly after 1:00 pm and he asked Tommy to meet both him and the rest of the directors in the boardroom within the next 30 minutes. Between snatched mouthfuls of pasta – my appetite had all but disappeared anyway – I had already hastily written his official letter of resignation and drove him back to the ground in his dark-blue Jaguar.

The team had been struggling from the start of that season and were languishing in 19th place, three points off the bottom of the table with eight points from 10 games. It was a situation that hardly helped his cause at that specific moment. There had been frequent mention in the papers as early as the start of September of 'internal unrest' and the chairman was quoted as 'perturbed at the moment but not terribly worried'. By the beginning of October, Tommy had ordered double training sessions without any rest days until Christmas. He had also banned the players from talking to the press, but the manager always did enough of that for the rest of them put together anyway.

With the benefit of hindsight, perhaps we should have waited and listened to the verdict of the chairman and his board. We will never know what their decision would have been if TD had decided to try to ride out the storm. But we didn't, and so came an end to Tommy's first managerial job after six years and nine months. It would be the longest period he ever spent at any club in his entire managerial career.

I waited in the club car park for over two hours, wondering but not particularly worrying where we would go from here and also musing how dear old Joe Mears would have dealt with the situation. It seemed that after 'reluctantly accepting' Tommy's decision, the board and he had all shared a bottle or two of champagne.

As Tommy emerged, Mr Pratt was already issuing a statement. Part of it read: 'No pressure was brought to bear on Tommy, although his suspension wasn't unrelated to his resignation. We were not pleased about that as it was something derogatory to Chelsea Football Club.'

Tommy's response as he sprinted out of the office side door was to jump into the front passenger seat and call out to the waiting newsmen, 'Six pm at my house!'

Not surprisingly, our lounge was packed with the media at the appointed hour. After serving drinks and snacks, I eavesdropped at the door to hear my husband declare, 'I didn't even know there was a case going on against me, but the suspension persuaded me that this is as good a time as any to make a fresh start.'

He may well have been right. Tommy's last act as the manager of Chelsea had been to select the team for the match at Leeds United the following afternoon. They lost 7–0.

In the programme notes for Chelsea's home game against Everton the next Saturday, 14 October, the club issued an official statement that said: 'Mr Docherty knew that his case was being dealt with by the Football Association and that he could have asked for a personal hearing.'

Tommy later admitted that this was true but, as on so many occasions in either his personal or professional life, he believed that sweeping problems under an imaginary carpet would make them go away.

Despite the hurried manner of his farewell, it wasn't too much of a shock to me. In fact, I think we were both slightly surprised he had stayed there for as long as he did after Joe's death. Tommy missed Joe's guidance, his utter devotion to the club and the carte blanche his old chairman had always afforded him. But then I came to suspect there was more to it than met my innocent eye. Some time after Tommy's resignation, I discovered from a close friend that a concerned Chelsea board of directors and his own colleagues knew all about Tommy's liaison with Maria. Indeed, it seemed they had known for considerably longer than I had.

My mind then went back to the letter I'd received in March 1965, which told me Tommy had been seeing one of the Chelsea players' wives. Had that been true and had the board known? Was that why Tommy and I had been packed off to Cannes for an unscheduled mid-season break by Joe Mears? So many unanswered questions, but then I suppose there always will be when your life is inextricably linked to a partner capable of such deception.

The following day, prior to starting his four-week sentence, I assumed that Tommy would defiantly want to go to a match. Instead, he suggested that we should take Peter to Cheshunt Zoo. It was surreal enough for *me* not to be attending a match or at least nervously waiting for the result on the radio, so I could only imagine how Tommy felt. As we left the aquarium and headed hand-in-hand for the car park, I remember thinking that my young son and I had just spent the afternoon in the confused company of a fish out of water.

The massive amount of publicity that Tommy's resignation generated convinced me that there would be no need for him to go searching for work. Quite the opposite, I thought, because the newspapers were doing it for him. But I had to bolster his clearly bruised morale by telling him that other managers must be 'shaking in their shoes' to know that he would shortly be available for employment. I could tell he was finding it difficult to share my confidence when, almost as a welcome distraction, a large black limousine drew up at our gate on the Tuesday morning to take us on the funniest 48-hour journey of our lives.

The chauffeur delivered a letter from a gentleman called George Latis, which explained that he represented John Pateras, an executive director of the Greek club Olympiakos. It was an invitation for us to meet Mr Latis at his apartment in town and to bring an overnight bag with us before boarding a flight on a private jet to Athens that very afternoon. Tommy and I glanced at one another, laughed aloud and thought, 'Why the hell not?'

The mysterious Mr Latis actually turned out to be a Scotsman with a Greek mother and he was charm personified. My solitary stipulation was that we should be accompanied by our solicitor, Harry Solomon, in case any contractual discussions should happen to take place. Mr Latis smiled and told us that there were plenty of spare seats.

Harry, who wore a permanent hangdog expression and yet was one of the most amusing men I ever knew, was already waiting for us in the departure lounge. The food during the four-hour flight was delicious, except Harry was an orthodox Jew and refused to eat anything except endless bars of chocolate throughout the entire two-day trip. Mr Latis, on the other hand, spent the duration of the journey 'selling' Olympiakos to Tommy.

On arrival in Athens, we were met by and introduced to Mr Pateras, whisked away in a presidential-style motorcade to a marina and taken on board an enormous yacht. We were escorted into a room and, as Harry and I stood discreetly by the door, Tommy was formally introduced by the Olympiakos executive to a semi-circle of very serious-looking men. In fact, it was all so serious that Harry and I could barely contain our laughter. Olympiakos were playing at home that night and, because TD was banned under FIFA rules from entering the stadium, Harry and I were despatched as scouts to report back to the potential new manager. To be honest, I don't think our combined match analysis swayed his judgement one way or another.

I did understand they had a professional agenda but, nevertheless, our hosts were delightful. That evening and throughout the following day, we were taken to see the Acropolis, dined and smashed plates in traditional style at one of the top restaurants in Athens and danced in a fabulous nightclub. There seemed to be a bouquet of flowers waiting for me everywhere we went and a puzzled young man was even sent off to buy Harry's dinner.

But we could both sense that Tommy didn't seem interested in accepting the post. Or any other for that matter. Worryingly, his lifelong love for football seemed to have suffered as a result of his suspension. Maybe it was the frustration of what might have been with that fine young team at Chelsea, maybe it was the belief that he was a victim of circumstances. Or maybe it was the last remaining embers of his affair with Maria. I knew our marriage was back on track and probably stronger than ever, but I was also starting to realise that I had a severely depressed husband on my hands.

When Tommy asked me if I thought he should take the job, I knew that he had lost some of his assertiveness. I couldn't remember the last time he had sought my advice on any aspect of his career. They were offering an awful lot of money, roughly the equivalent of £8,000 a year, and I hesitated for a moment before replying, 'You don't seem sure and all I can say is, if in doubt, don't.'

He smiled and said, 'But we could end up in Rotherham, for God's sake!'

His mind was made up that night, if not before, and Harry only had two problems the next morning before our flight home. The first was having to eat yet more chocolate for breakfast and the second was to be aware of Greeks bearing gifts. He tried in vain to convince the persuasive Mr Pateras and his financial director that Tommy wasn't holding the club to ransom, because every genuine refusal to sign the contract lying on the table was greeted with a slightly increased offer in salary, until it simply became silly. Having said that, it never reached the stage of becoming irresistible. This was a man obviously used to getting what he wanted but Tommy equally clearly didn't want to move to Greece.

If I had been in any doubt about TD's fragile morale, then I became certain when his suspension finally elapsed and he failed to jump at the first opportunity to attend a match. I had imagined that the prisoner would have been mentally ticking off the days until the end of his sentence. But he missed the following midweek and Saturday fixtures too, seemingly content to quietly sit in front of the television, licking his wounds and watching a succession of old movies. He didn't even want to know the full-time scores. His exile, for some reason I failed to understand, had now become self-imposed. I gently coaxed but never pushed him, merely suggesting that it wouldn't do any harm to be seen in his normal environment.

But it was another week before Ron Goodman invited him to a match at Leyton Orient and he came home resembling a religious convert who had seen the light. Or floodlights. Apparently, he had been given a rousing reception by the crowd at Brisbane Road that night. The football animal had returned to his natural habitat and it seemed to have rekindled his confidence. Until that month of enforced separation from Tommy's one true love, self-esteem was the one commodity I would never have believed could desert him.

Tommy was being associated with different clubs on a daily newspaper basis – many of which didn't even appear to have an immediate managerial vacancy – but the first genuine offer apart from Olympiakos came, of course, from Rotherham United. Tommy somewhat sceptically drove up to meet the chairman, Eric Purshouse, on Wednesday, 22 November, and came back some seven hours later as the ebullient manager of that struggling Second Division side.

He had accepted an annual contract of £5,750, a huge financial undertaking for such a small club. Once again, I hadn't been consulted but I had to admire the club's ambition and Tommy's rediscovered optimism. I was also acutely aware that moving from the bright theatre lights of London to the sleepy street lights of South Yorkshire was always going to be a culture shock. But, after 19 years together and an enormous marital hiccup, I genuinely felt that I was back where I belonged. And that was wherever my husband happened to be. Nothing else, apart from my children, really mattered.

So, once again, I phoned my pals at Pickfords to warn them that we were on the move. I spent whatever time I could in the next two months regularly driving up to Yorkshire looking at a succession of houses while Tommy stayed in a hotel near Millmoor, Rotherham's ground. Finally, I found 71 Hallam Road, Rotherham. It filled an essential part of our criteria of being within a 20-minute drive of the club, so I arranged for Tommy to meet me there. He never wanted to look until I had found what we always called 'a definite possibility' and, in all our years together, he never once disagreed with my final choice. We moved in on 29 January 1968.

However, I wasn't to know that this was the beginning of our nomadic period, when I started to wonder at times if it was actually worth unpacking – and when I realised one morning that I knew the number for Pickfords by heart.

CHAPTER 10

ON THE ROAD AGAIN

To travel hopefully is a better thing than to arrive.
ROBERT LOUIS STEVENSON (1850–94)

There isn't too much to say about the 11 months that we spent in South Yorkshire because nothing really happened. I know Tommy had a genuine vision of transforming a struggling team from the backwaters of English football to the absolute pinnacle of the European game. Try not to laugh too loudly at the thought of Rotherham United locking horns with Real Madrid and AC Milan. Many others have since tried and similarly failed with far greater finances at their disposal.

It was part of my husband's personal manifesto but, as with so many idealistic politicians, that was all it could ever be. An impossible dream. Much later, I gather it became part of his after-dinner repertoire when Tommy would joke, 'I promised the chairman I would take them out of Division Two and I did. We were relegated...'

They finished second from bottom, and guess which team

were directly above them, avoiding a similar fate by four points? Preston North End. Yet I have no wish to denigrate that friendly little Yorkshire town or indeed the club. After all, they shared the same ambition and lived the same dream, but I always felt that Rotherham was no more than a brief detour in Tommy's career. I didn't mind our period of self-imposed solitude there. After all the headlines, it was almost a welcome breather. In many ways, Rotherham reminded me of a less successful Preston. They were both places where the club was part of the community and vice versa.

I had decided that both Catherine and Tom should have the kind of stability in their education that Tommy's career was clearly starting to lack. So, with some reluctance, they were sent off to boarding schools, Catherine to St Joseph's Convent in Stafford and Tom to St Joseph's College, Dumfries. Fortunately, their inherited adaptability enabled them to settle in quickly and with Michael doing well at Burnely, I really only had three-year-old Peter to keep me occupied. Dad, who had naturally moved with us, was still on hand to help out in that department. TD, on the other hand, had rapidly resumed his habit of attending as many matches as humanly possible, although he religiously reserved every Thursday evening to take me out for a meal. Perhaps because that was one of the days of the week that you could *almost* guarantee there would never be a game on of some sort or another.

The choice of restaurant in Rotherham was rather limited compared to our life in London but we would dine, share a bottle of wine and slowly put the world to rights. The world of football, of course. This was Tommy's universe, after all. Little else outside football existed. I'm sure he must have noticed that Peter started playschool after a severe bout of measles that summer and that Catherine broke three toes while attempting to play football in the back garden with her brothers. It's just that, to Tommy, those kinds of incidents were almost incidental in his life.

There were certainly no public recriminations or lasting regrets on either side when Tommy gave Rotherham a month's notice on 31 October 1968. As far as the club were concerned, their departing manager had put them on the sporting map. Also, among his many transfer dealings, Tommy had bought a young centre-half called Dave Watson from Notts County for £500 and sold him nine months later to Sunderland for £100,000. Watson would go on to play 65 times for England and Rotherham's payday represented an enormous profit for any club in that era. Besides, Tommy had been offered the manager's job at struggling First Division Queens Park Rangers on £6,750 a year. I can't deny that I was delighted we were on our way back to London.

From sharing several seasons of post-match drinks with his peers and finding so many of them fearful, frustrated or simply resentful, nobody was more aware than Tommy of how fortunate he had been to have worked under his first two chairmen, Joe Mears at Chelsea and then Eric Purshouse at Rotherham. Both did what they did for the love of the game, and not out of some sadly misguided sense of self-importance. Both allowed Tommy to get on and do the job he had been hired to do. Their brief couldn't have been more straightforward. Here's your salary and here's your budget.

Wheel and deal in the transfer market as best you can but preferably in the black, coach the players, pick the team and, if we win trophies, that's a bonus. Happy, innocent days before the initials FC were effectively replaced by plc. When a points total meant far more than a profit margin. Call me nostalgic if you must but please never accuse me of envy. I was involved in football at the best of times.

Perhaps by the law of averages, Tommy was about to discover the antithesis of the non-interventionist club chairman. His name was Jim Gregory and he happened to be in charge of QPR. Totally in charge. He wore very loud suits, smoked ludicrously large cigars and possessed an inflated ego bigger than a hot-air balloon. Now I think about it, that's precisely what he was – a sort of human zeppelin. Had I previously met Mr Gregory, I would have called Pickfords and asked them to place one of their smaller vehicles on permanent standby at the training ground to collect my husband for when he and Mr Gregory fell out, as they inevitably would. QPR as a club was simply not big enough for the both of them.

In the end, I didn't need to call Pickfords. I was still house-hunting in London four weeks after Tommy's appointment when he told me to call off the search. Naturally, I asked why. 'Because there's no point.' he grimaced, before adding, 'I've just resigned.' He had been the manager for exactly 28 days. Jim Gregory's team were relegated without trace that season, winning just four games out of 42, and I was sure it couldn't have happened to a nicer chairman.

Yet it was only in the months that rapidly followed that we ruefully realised QPR was merely a frying pan. A new consortium had taken over at struggling Second Division side Aston Villa. Just before Christmas, they offered Tommy the manager's post. Yet again, without discussing it with me, he accepted on a salary of £8,000 a year.

The fire that he was about to unwittingly jump into was being gleefully stoked by a tough businessman called Doug Ellis, a chairman who didn't seem to mind controversy. I don't know who first gave him the nickname of 'Deadly Doug' for his subsequent penchant of sacking a succession of managers, but he always seemed to me to brush off the notoriety. I remember an exhausted TD arriving home in Rotherham late on the Saturday night after his first week in charge at Villa. He slumped into a chair and said, 'They don't have a reserve team, they've never even *heard* of a youth scheme and as for the first team – oh, my God!'

I could only help by supporting him, listening patiently and instantly switching my house-hunting focus from London to Birmingham, eventually settling on 158 Rosemary Hill Road, Sutton Coldfield. It was within the requisite journey time from the ground and I loved that house the moment I set eyes on it. In the meantime, Tommy did an enormous amount of groundwork in the ensuing weeks and months, organising national scouts, initiating reserve and youth sides and constantly wheeling and dealing in the transfer market in an attempt to improve the inadequate first team.

Villa managed to stave off relegation that season, finishing eight points above the drop zone in 18th position. I don't know exactly when Tommy realised he was fighting a losing battle, but when Villa lost seven and drew two of their opening nine

League matches of the 1969/70 season, to lie firmly rooted to the foot of the table, Tommy didn't need telling that he was in deep trouble. But the press, bless their little poisonous pens, began to apply the pressure anyway. When Chairman Doug called Tommy in for the dreaded vote of confidence, it was a sure sign that trouble lay ahead. 'Don't worry, Tommy, I'm right behind you,' he told his manager.

TD replied, 'That's fine, Mr Chairman, but I would rather you were right in front of me so that I can see what you're up to.'

Apparently, Doug laughed – but all I could visualise was the smile of an assassin. Villa had already been knocked out of the FA Cup 1–0 in a third-round replay by Charlton Athletic and, on the morning of Monday, 16 January 1970, after losing 5–3 at home to Portsmouth at the weekend, the club called an emergency board meeting. Never exactly an encouraging sign.

Villa had won just four of their 26 matches that season and the writing was literally on the walls outside the ground. Tommy walked past the spray-painted, obscene graffiti on his way to attend and deliver a progress report – I remember thinking, 'That wouldn't take too long' – before returning to his office to await what we both anticipated would be the inevitable outcome. At 4:30 pm he was summoned to see the board again, where he was sacked for the first time in his life. He had been there for 13 months. 'More fool them,' I told Tommy when he called to give me their decision.

Still, it wasn't all bad news that week as Michael, at the age of 19, had just been appointed the captain of Burnley in the First Division. For days, I found myself lying awake at night bursting with equal measures of pride and indignation! Villa were relegated to the Third Division at the end of that season – along with Preston North End.

All these years and generally empty-handed seasons at Villa Park later, I find myself thinking that if only the likes of Doug Ellis and so many faceless football directors could realise the importance of continuity, of giving a manager that most precious of commodities: time. Perhaps more than ever today, the main item on the agenda is instant success. Why can't they realise that it doesn't exist? It never has and it never will. I remember that, by general consensus in the early months of 1990, Alex Ferguson was teetering on the edge of dismissal at Manchester United. The rest, as they say, is history.

I also recall Doug being ousted in a boardroom coup about a decade earlier before regaining control at the club some two seasons later. If I'm not mistaken, Aston Villa won the League Championship followed by the European Cup in his absence. I'm only a woman, I was only ever a loyal wife, so consider me biased or bitter if you must, but those statistics tell me all I need to know. Doug's survival for so long at the helm of Aston Villa (he finally sold the club to American billionaire Randy Lerner in 2006) is proof that it's not only the strong who survive, it's quite often the stubborn as well.

So, Tommy and I were on the road again. Three houses in 27 months and once again looking for a new town. Life with Tommy was many things, occasionally with too many strings, but it was never, ever dull.

He was inundated with various offers and, just 12 days after his dismissal, my husband flew to Malaga to briefly consider and equally rapidly dismiss one proposal before catching another plane on to northern Portugal where, without even the formality of an official interview, he was asked to become the coach of Porto. They had offered him a non-negotiable annual salary of £8,500, but I didn't really believe for a moment that he would accept the job – until he phoned on the evening of Thursday, 5 February to tell me that it had been too good to turn down. And, by the way, could I fly out the next day to look at a choice of several houses and apartments? The club had reserved a ticket for me, he said, to be collected at the check-in desk at Heathrow. After a frantic few hours of arranging childcare and packing some suitable clothes, I somehow found myself the next day in Oporto.

Tommy and a chauffeur met me on arrival. I soon discovered that nothing was too much trouble for the wife of the revered 'Meester Doc', as those delightful, football-crazy people referred to him. After a hectic tour of five properties the following day, I eventually chose a beautiful four-bedroom beachside villa in the nearby coastal resort of Miramar as our next home.

But, for once, I insisted to Tommy that we should retain our house in Sutton Coldfield as I had the strangest feeling that this would be yet another short-lived adventure. Recent experience had taught me to be cautious. I think Tommy was seeking to replicate those early, exciting days at Chelsea, except that none of the boardroom power-brokers wanted to play his kind of ball game any more.

Just 48 hours later, I was back in Birmingham, where I suddenly realised, with an equal mixture of excitement and trepidation, that there was so much to do. I still couldn't quite comprehend what Tommy had done. In those days, foreign teams had local coaches and local players. They didn't employ foreigners.

In slightly over 20 years, I had become the proud mother of four lovely children, moved from Girvan to Preston, on to London, Rotherham and then Birmingham, next stop Oporto, suffered a miscarriage, lived through my mother's death, survived major surgery, faced a potential divorce and so much more than I sometimes cared to remember or even believe. And I was more than conscious of the fact that the meter was still running. I mentioned the rollercoaster ride of a lifetime earlier in my recollections but it's only now, as I continue to commit my thoughts to paper, that I finally begin to realise exactly how many twists and turns that remarkable journey would take before I finally jumped off. Actually that's wrong. In the end, I was heartlessly pushed.

Prior to returning to Portugal with Peter almost exactly seven weeks later at the end of March, I made a multitude of arrangements – and two mistakes. Dad would happily look after the house in the Midlands, while our youngest child was naturally accepted as a pupil at the local British school, which would also provide twice-weekly evening lessons in Portuguese for Tommy and myself. Michael continued to thrive at Burnley, and Catherine and Tom would excitedly fly over to Oporto during their three annual holidays from boarding school. I was confident that I had thought of everything.

The mistakes? Firstly, I had booked the passage of my husband's brand-new maroon XJ6 Jaguar by sea with the name of Tommy Docherty prominently attached to the necessary paperwork. From Liverpool Docks. When we were asked to come and collect the vehicle from the container ship at the port in Lisbon, the crude carvings made from penknives and keys of 'LFC', 'KOP RULES' and 'SHANKLY IS GOD' that greeted us were some of the more polite slogans scratched across the previously pristine bodywork of my husband's pride and joy. And this was *before* Tommy was manager at Manchester United. I told you earlier of Tommy's attitude to the Welsh, but I think the Scousers leapfrogged to runners-up in his all-time list after that nasty episode.

My second oversight was that I had viewed the villa and surrounding, secluded beach in the middle of the afternoon and it had all seemed so idyllic. When we were woken up at just after 5:00 am on our first morning in this new country by what sounded like at least 100 of our nearest neighbour's cockerels greeting the dawn, I realised that packing an alarm clock had been completely unnecessary.

Porto performed very well for the remainder of that season but were unable to loosen the stranglehold of the mighty and richer Benfica. A young Patrick Collins, later an award-winning sports journalist of the *Mail on Sunday*, came over for a few days to write a feature on Tommy's life in Portuguese football and it did wonders for my husband's morale. I think he dreaded being out of sight, out of mind, but we both knew that this was only ever going to be another station on our journey.

In fact, our lives in Portugal really just felt like an extended holiday. This feeling was thrown into stark relief when I received a letter from Dad telling me that Michael was seriously ill in hospital with glandular fever and jaundice. Not for the first time, I cursed the fact that we weren't on the telephone in our remote accommodation. Peter and I enthusiastically packed our bags to collect Michael from England and take him off for a recuperative fortnight in Benidorm, while Tommy set off for Mexico to work as a summariser for the BBC on the 1970 World Cup. The phone calls between our Spanish hotel and South America cost almost as much as the holiday.

The following season flew as quickly as my frequent trips back home to check on Michael's steady progress and visits to Catherine and Tom at their boarding schools. Yet I knew that our time in that lovely country would end by mutual consent when once again Porto predictably failed to break the Benfica monopoly and we finished in second place. Perhaps the Porto directors and fans were expecting miracles but even Tommy couldn't perform them on demand – apart from the memorable afternoon of 31 January 1971, when we were at home to the almost perennial Portuguese champions.

I didn't watch the games on TV or listen to them on the radio out there. Instead, I'd wait anxiously at home for Tommy's return after a match, listening out for the telltale grunts of disappointment or chirpy whistles of success as he arrived home. This time, I didn't have to bother. As I was sitting in the lounge reading a book while Peter enjoyed a siesta upstairs, something made me glance through the panoramic windows towards the shore. And that was when I saw them. About 50 fully clothed men, women and children dancing and singing in the sea in the middle of winter. They had simultaneously noticed me and began to noisily descend on the house, letting me know that Porto had beaten Benfica 4–0. In their eyes, 'Meester Doc' was now officially God.

I'm not sure why I let them all in the house, but it took me a while to get them out again – and not before finding one of the wringing-wet fanatics in the downstairs bathroom pouring Tommy's very expensive aftershave over his hair and the entire upper half of his body. I could only assume that he wanted to smell like his hero. I learned a long time ago never to underestimate the devotion of the average football fan. That slightly surreal experience was one of the reasons I finally decided that the villa was totally impractical. We had no telephone and, once Tommy had left for the day in his resprayed car, no transport. There were few shops locally and just one restaurant. What if there was an emergency? What if we ever *lost* 4–0 to Benfica? How would I cope with 50 fans rampaging towards the house in that situation?

Tommy mentioned my concern to the club the following morning and, possibly due in part to the previous day's result, we had been installed in a plush split-level apartment in the city centre in time for dinner that evening. The villa, we were told, remained at our disposal should we wish to spend weekends there. Still, it wasn't enough. The pull of home was too much, so at the end of that season Tommy and Porto parted company and we returned to Birmingham.

Within a week of moving back to England, Tommy was in such a depressed state that I occasionally wondered if another *femme fatale* was hovering on some distant, unknown horizon. And then I would silently chastise myself with the realisation that, for the first time in his professional career, a new season was imminent and Tommy didn't have a job. He refused to contemplate signing on the dole. In fact, he refused to even leave the lounge in case anybody happened to call with the prospect of employment. Then, three insufferable weeks later, the phone rang for roughly three-hundredths of a second before Tommy answered it. His ex-Arsenal colleague Terry Neill, the youngster who had inadvertently been partially responsible for his departure from Highbury, was on the other end. He had recently been appointed manager of Hull City in the Second Division and was calling to ask Tommy if he was available to help him out. The club could only afford £3,000 a year but, champing at the bit, TD agreed on the spot, put the phone down and asked me to prepare to move lock, stock and barrel to Hull.

I urged him not to be so stupid. I told him that he was not an assistant manager and that we should stay in Sutton Coldfield until he received a more attractive offer. For the first time in our lives, we now had enough savings to survive for a reasonable period of time. Tommy stood and listened to my logic for as long as his feet would allow him and then, when he thought I had finished, ran upstairs, threw some clothes into a suitcase, kissed me sideways as he sprinted out of the door and jumped into his car.

I knew it was a drug and he was an addict. An incurable one. I can only smile now at the distant memory of watching him drive into the darkness as I stood at the front door, shouting at the rapidly disappearing tail lights, 'By the way, where the hell is Hull?'

CHAPTER 11

TO HULL AND BACK

*None climbs so high as he who knows not whither
he is going.*

OLIVER CROMWELL (1599–1658)

For the three or so meandering months that Tommy commuted to North Yorkshire from Birmingham, we reverted to our earliest courting days. Catching rare glimpses of one another on truncated weekends, with me worrying if this was all there was, when, everything suddenly changed with an unexpected phone call from the Scottish Football Association on a cold September night in 1971. Tommy had been invited to become the manager of the national team on an annual salary of £7,000.

There had been mild speculation linking him with the post but we had learned long ago never to trust newspaper talk, especially where TD was concerned. But this was official. Tommy was delirious. I was dubious. Don't misunderstand me. I appreciate that it was and remains a great accolade, but to my mind it's a job for a man of a certain age, someone who is semi-retired and with a bit more experience. An elder statesman of the game. Not Tommy.

For one of the few times in our marriage, I totally disagreed with Tommy's next decision. Within a week of taking the job, Tommy was insistent that we should move back north of the border, purely because the manager of Scotland couldn't be seen to be living in England. Why, he reasoned, encourage criticism and alienate perhaps the most patriotic football supporters in the world if you can avoid it? It was a perfectly valid argument and, although I thought I had far more practical reasons for staying put, I knew his mind was firmly made up.

For my part, I didn't want to continue to disrupt the early years of Peter's education by moving yet again. I was extremely reluctant to sell our house in Sutton Coldfield and, apart from Tom at boarding school in Dumfries, it would place Michael and Catherine too far away from regular visiting distance. It had been quicker to commute from Portugal! By now, my only daughter had completed her education and, as nearly all her friends were living in the Midlands and she had loved it from the moment we first moved there, she decided to settle in the area and quickly found a flat and a job as a qualified swimming instructor at a leisure centre close to our Sutton Coldfield home.

And that's what it should have remained: our home. Shortly after moving into a small and depressing rented flat on the outskirts of Glasgow city centre in order to start searching for a suitable property, it occurred to me that, while *we* were moving up north to Scotland, most of the country's best players had already moved south to England. This meant that Birmingham would have been an ideal base for Tommy to travel to anywhere in the country to watch a match. If Tommy staying in England upset people in Scotland, I couldn't have seen it worrying him too much. He'd spent most of his career ignoring public disapproval. It was water off a Doc's back. But, Tommy was insistent that we go back to Scotland.

If I was completely against the idea, I was astonished when my own father, as proud a Scotsman as you could find, told me that he didn't want to move back to his home country either. As three of my kids were now grown up, I think Dad had come to see himself as something of a non-paying lodger in our lives, and the constant moving from place to place, taking him with us each time, only reinforced that fact to him. I think he decided that it was time to stay put and let us move on. Sometimes of an evening, as I watched him cutting up the sports pages of the newspapers in his unofficial role of Tommy Docherty archivist, I realised that in our own ways neither Dad nor I had ever really come to terms with the loss of my mother. I didn't want to lose him now, just because he thought he was of no practical use to the family any more. Of course, I didn't even consider discussing such concerns with Tommy. If it wasn't to do with football, it wasn't something he'd have understood.

So my dear dad moved back to Preston to live in a council flat, close to where my two wee sisters could keep an eye on him for the rest of his dwindling days. I stifled many a tear while reluctantly accepting his decision. I wouldn't have let him leave at all had I known that I would never see him again. After moving back to Scotland, Tommy and I saw much more of each other, a pleasant side-effect of the fact that he was no longer a club manager. But my close observation of my hyperactive husband only reinforced my conviction that he was in the wrong job. He was 43 years old and not even in the prime of his managerial career. Life seemed to be moving at half-speed. To me, it resembled the close season – that time of year Tommy had always considered wasteful – and now it had become a virtually permanent state of existence. I was convinced there wouldn't be nearly enough to occupy him, that he would miss the daily involvement and weekly challenge of league football and it didn't take long for my suspicions to be proved correct.

One morning, several weeks into his new job, Tommy asked me if he could take a loaf of bread to his office with him. When he added that it didn't matter if it was slightly stale, I was perturbed and asked him if the SFA wasn't even providing him with lunch. 'Of course they are,' he replied, 'it's just that I like to feed the pigeons on the window ledge of my office in the afternoon. It passes the time.'

I laughed before realising that, bloody hell, he was serious!

Yet, although I may not have agreed with Tommy's decision, it didn't alter the fact that the boy who had literally grappled his way out of the crime-infested Gorbals of Glasgow was now the football manager of his country. But my delight was tempered by the realisation that such was the paucity of top-class Scottish players in that era that Tommy could select his squad in the space of just one short morning at his desk, presumably spending the rest of the day handing out stale bread to his cooing friends outside the office window.

Football is a game of coincidences, so I shouldn't have been too surprised to discover that Tommy's first match in charge was a European Championship qualifier at Hampden Park on 13 October against Portugal. Or indeed that the date happened to be the anniversary of Mum's funeral, when Dad and I had persuaded my husband to go and play for his country. Seventeen years on, they managed to win 2–1 with goals from the Derby County duo of John O'Hare and Archie Gemmill. Four weeks later, in the same competition, they also beat Belgium 1–0 in Aberdeen with a fifth-minute goal by O'Hare. However, three away defeats in the group – to both of those countries and Denmark before Tommy took over – had already inflicted irreparable damage. Tommy rightly knew that Scotland would not make it to the 1972 Finals, which were eventually won by the old West Germany. Instead, he set his sights on building a team for the 1974 World Cup Finals to be held in West Germany.

By the time Tommy became Scotland manager, my wee seven-year-old boy Peter was a seasoned traveller. I didn't think anything could faze him. Until we moved to Glasgow, that is. When he started being frequently sick in the morning and I was called by the school to collect him three times in the opening few weeks of the term, I consulted our new doctor. Having inspected my son, he arranged an appointment with a consultant paediatrician. After various tests I was told that, unless we removed Peter from his present environment, the likelihood was that he would develop an ulcer.

An ulcer. At seven years old. That was it. In no time at all I'd found us a new place outside the city centre, 9 Windsor Gardens, in the seaside town of Largs. It's on the Ayrshire coast – I had almost come full circle, after all – and Peter attended a school run by the same religious order, the Marist Brothers, that had been so successfully teaching my second son in Dumfries. But Tom, home for his Christmas holidays, was about to discover that religious sectarianism wasn't something confined just to Scottish cities.

As a young and naturally shy newcomer in the small town, and the son of Tommy Docherty, Tom found himself singled out for attention by a gang of local youths as he walked home alone one evening. The latest Scotland squad had been announced earlier in the day for the forthcoming friendly international against Holland in Rotterdam on 1 December and the presence of several Celtic (i.e. Catholic) players in the squad obviously upset these possibly Rangers (i.e. Protestant) youths from Largs. Knowing that Tom was the son of a prominent Catholic football man such as Tommy Docherty was all the encouragement those young bigots needed and they set about Tom.

G.K. Chesterton once defined bigotry as 'the anger of men who have no opinions', but when our son staggered through the front door, badly bruised and with blood pouring from a nasty gash just below his left eye, his father certainly *did* possess an opinion. He was so angry that I had to restrain him from going in search of the culprits. I could imagine the headlines and asked him how it would look if the Scottish manager was involved in a street fight. But I'm fairly sure I know how *they* would have looked if I had allowed Tommy to confront them. The lads of Largs, no matter their number, would have been well advised to avoid the enraged grown-up from the Gorbals in a dark alley.

Despite the periods of enforced inactivity, Tommy appeared to generally enjoy his new job. It may have been the fact that he had a marginally better generation of players to choose from than most of his predecessors, or perhaps it was the therapeutic company of the pigeons. Whatever it was, in preparation for their forthcoming World Cup campaign, the squad embarked on a brief tour of South America in the summer of 1972. The highlight of the three-match trip, which included draws against Yugoslavia and Czechoslovakia, was losing only 1–0 to Brazil in front of 130,000 spectators at the Maracana Stadium in Rio de Janeiro.

Scotland began their quest to qualify for the 1974 World Cup with successive victories against Denmark, 4–1 in Copenhagen on 18 October, and 2–0 at Hampden Park four weeks later. The first goal in Glasgow that night was scored after only two minutes by a young Celtic striker to whom Tommy had given his international debut as a substitute against Belgium the previous November. It had been the first of a richly deserved 102 caps for Kenneth Mathieson Dalglish.

Ten days after that home win, my dad died on Saturday, 25 November, four days before what would have been his 72nd birthday. We took him to his final resting place, beside his wife at Doune Cemetery in Girvan. His Requiem Mass was held at the Sacred Heart, the same church in which Tommy and I had been married. It feels the most awful thing to have to admit, but I wasn't nearly as distraught about my dad's death as I had been when my mum passed away. I was very upset, of course, but the sense of loss simply wasn't as all-consuming.

However, my conscience was eased slightly by the realisation that Mum had always been my role model, the one person I could turn to about absolutely anything. I had also been considerably younger when she died. Life held fewer surprises after everything I had been through since. Furthermore, I had always felt since 1954 that her surviving husband had spent the ensuing 18 years merely waiting to join her again. Whether that's true or not, I know he maintained a pretence that I occasionally wondered in later years if it was possible I may have inherited.

Less than a month later, on Tuesday, 19 December, I received the phone call that would change our lives forever.

It was from Matt Busby, who had become a director at Manchester United. We had a pleasant chat before I explained that Tommy was on his way to an evening function at Norwich City's ground, Carrow Road, that evening. Matt left his number and asked if TD would be kind enough to ring him when he arrived home. He was back in the house considerably earlier than I had expected, because, on his way to East Anglia, Tommy decided to detour to Sutton Coldfield and drop in on Catherine, who by now was 18 years old and sharing a larger flat with two girlfriends.

It was just as well he did. He found her with what was later diagnosed as a severe viral infection, packed her into the car and headed straight back to Scotland. Anxious not to worry me, Tommy didn't phone until he reached a petrol station about five miles from home, explained the situation and said that I should call the doctor and prepare a room for our daughter. Within a matter of minutes, she was being fussed over, the antibiotics were being prepared and she was safely tucked up in bed. Only then did I remember to mention that Matt had called earlier that evening.

I casually suggested that he could have seen a young Scottish player and was calling to recommend him. I didn't know Frank O'Farrell had been sacked as the Manchester United manager earlier that day. TD obviously had heard the news. As I looked at him for his reaction, the blood visibly drained from his face. It was one of the few times in his life I'd seen Tommy speechless. When he did finally find the words to tell me about Frank's dismissal, it was my turn to not know what to say. I felt nauseous and couldn't complete a coherent sentence. My hand was shaking as I passed Tommy the piece of paper with the number on it and I held my breath as he immediately dialled it. I would normally leave Tommy alone if he was conducting business at home. On this occasion, I wouldn't have left the lounge if there had been a fire raging in the kitchen.

I could tell that from Tommy's expression and the tears starting to well in his eyes that the news was good. I watched as he listened to one of the legends of the game offering him the opportunity to follow in his own footsteps. As soon as he hung up, Tommy and I shrieked and danced around the lounge like demented teenagers. Tommy had been saving a bottle of champagne to crack open when Scotland qualified for the World Cup, but we soon polished that off. When Tommy finally went off to bed I stayed up for a while, going in to check on Catherine and sitting quietly while I tried to unravel my scrambled thoughts.

I found myself crying tears of pride as I looked back over what we'd been through to get to this point in our lives, the seemingly endless days of deprivation, the tin baths and low-ceilinged larders, lost wages and pawn shops, sleeping in tracksuits and waking up laughing, losing my milk and finding my engagement ring, a spinal operation and German pregnancy. And then my thoughts drifted to my parents.

They were both gone now and I particularly regretted the fact that my dad hadn't lived to see it. He admired Matt Busby so much and would have loved to have socialised with the great man. They both came from the same granite-hard part of the world in Lanarkshire and I was sure they would have enjoyed one another's company. But I also knew my mum would have been incredibly proud. Tommy had reached the peak of his profession and we had made it there as a team. My husband was always the first to acknowledge that fact. He once said, 'I'll get the points and you look after the pounds. You are so very special to me that it would take a welder to separate us!'

I also spared more than a passing thought for Frank and Anne O'Farrell and the trauma they must have been going through. Our elation was matched only by their despair. I remembered feeding Frank in our tiny kitchen in Preston all those years ago after Anne's miscarriage and my current contentment was tempered by the realisation that football can be such a ruthless game. I found myself wishing they had been total strangers instead of such good friends.

As daylight broke, I was still thinking, smiling and simultaneously crying when Peter, whose godparents by a cruel twist of fate happen to be Frank and Anne, stumbled downstairs in search of his breakfast. I excitedly told him that his dad was the new manager of Manchester United and, between noisy mouthfuls of cereal, he mumbled, 'That's great, Mum – but does it mean we'll be moving again?'

I laughed aloud at my wee boy, kissed him and picked up the phone to warn Pickfords.

Pretty soon the news was official. As of Friday, 22 December, Tommy Docherty was to be the new Manchester United manager, on an annual salary of £15,000.

With United's agreement, Tommy called Jimmy Aitken, the SFA's International Committee Chairman, and offered to continue managing the national side through the qualification process and hopefully into the 1974 World Cup. He was genuinely anxious to finish the job he'd started but I wasn't surprised when they declined the offer and appointed Willie Ormond as his replacement. How could they have been seen to publicly admit something that I had known for so long? That international management of any country is a part-time occupation.

I have to admit, I screamed with laughter just over two years later when TD came storming in one evening and told me that Ormond had been awarded the OBE for services to Scottish football, before adding, 'For getting them to the World Cup and then getting knocked out! Can you believe that? I should have got the O and at least part of the bloody B!'

Not surprisingly, given my considerable experience, it only

took me about a month to find The Elms on Hawley Lane, Hale Barns. It was outside our precondition of 20 minutes from the training ground, almost an hour in fact, but it was a 10-minute drive from Manchester Airport, off the main flight path and as irresistible as any property within our price range could ever be. It cost £27,950. I always remember how Tommy thought he had 'arrived' the first time he tried on his Crombie overcoat a decade earlier, but that beautiful house in the sleepy suburbs of Cheshire really was the culmination of our dreams. It represented everything we had scrimped and saved, borrowed and repaid and tirelessly worked together to achieve. Perhaps it's only possible to appreciate this if you have made the same kind of journey in your own life but, for the first few weeks, we used to go for long evening walks – around the house. There were rooms I would go into to clean and then realise nobody had been in there for a fortnight! I wanted everybody I knew to visit us just so that I could show them around. Not to show off but simply because I felt like a wee girl who had been given the biggest and best doll's house in the whole world.

The only disappointing aspect of the property was the back garden. It was large but comparatively humdrum. As I was trying to think what to do with it, Catherine came up to visit and provided the (expensive) answer. After no more than a glance, she suggested we should have a patio laid – with a swimming pool in the middle. I asked her if she thought her dad was Rockefeller but Tommy thought it was a fantastic idea, so I made the appropriate enquiries. It transpired that, at 35ft long and 15ft wide, it would cost just over £2,000. It turned out to be a very sound investment, apart from the prohibitive cost of heating it from a boiler in the double garage and friends questioning the logic of owning an outdoor pool in Manchester in the first place.

Because he had travelled so extensively in his career and disliked being too far away from work for more than a few days even in the summer, it was a perfect addition to the property for Tommy. On hot afternoons, we would occasionally stand in the pool, nibbling smoked salmon sandwiches and drinking chilled champagne. As an indulgent birthday present the following April, I even had small floodlights installed to enable him to have a midnight swim. I thought he deserved it.

We felt like millionaires and, compared to the early days of our marriage, we were. Once I had dreamed of central heating in the house and now we even had it in our own swimming pool in the garden.

Despite the various jobs in between, it was his time at Chelsea that had earned Tommy a reputation as something of a disciplinarian who loved to nurture young talent. He had also become known as a troubleshooter. Despite his conviction that he had been given the top job in the country, my husband was only too well aware that United was a club in steep decline – and that that was why he had been appointed in the first place. After all, apart from the almost seamless succession of Liverpool managers during their long period of domination, how many men are fortunate enough to inherit a successful side? I can only think of one – he did it twice and both times at the expense of my husband.

Dave Sexton took over at Chelsea and went on to win the FA Cup in 1970 and the European Cup Winners Cup the following season with the nucleus of the team that Tommy built in West London. Sexton was also to be one of the first names on the list of possible successors at Old Trafford during the hot summer of 1977, a period that I will obviously return to later.

Just how much of a decline United was in was something Tommy didn't realise until he took up his new role. The club was rotten to the core, riven by the internal squabbling of too many players long past their sell-by dates. Maybe he should have called Frank O'Farrell to sound out the situation but, apart from feeling guilty that we should benefit from his demise, I don't think that Frank or anybody else could have possibly dissuaded Tommy from taking up the challenge. It was irresistible.

Anyway, I've always believed the deposed boss was too nice a man to have been able to deal with that particular situation. It needed a more ruthless character, devoid of emotion, to make some very unpopular decisions. Too many of those players were United legends surviving on reputation alone. No fewer than half the team that had been humiliated 5–0 at bottom-placed Crystal Palace in Frank's last match in charge on 16 December had memorably won the European Cup less than five seasons earlier. But they were now an ageing team and they were either unwilling or unable to accept the inevitable passage of time. Perhaps because he had retired from playing himself at the age of 32, TD couldn't understand the reluctance of others to similarly call it a day. Knowing when to go; that's the trick, they say.

Fortunately for my husband, and not really surprisingly, Bobby Charlton was the notable exception. One of Manchester United and English football's greatest ambassadors, Bobby wasted no time in informing the new manager that this current season would be his last. To paraphrase the words of the famous film director Billy Wilder, he might have added that, if he'd known that campaign was going to be his swansong, he would have bet on a different swan. United weren't just flirting with relegation, they were going steady.

Charlton's decision prevented Tommy from having to make an even harder one himself and I know he was always grateful to him for that. It was other members of that crumbling empire that would induce insomnia in my husband, the two most significant being George Best and Denis Law. In the months that followed, Tommy's behaviour towards those two Old Trafford legends provided a perfect if unnerving example of the Jekyll and Hyde character that Tommy had become, or perhaps always was. Like the game itself – a man of two halves.

At the beginning of December, an exasperated United had placed Best on the transfer list and suspended him for a fortnight for, as they termed it, 'persistent truancy'. Fittingly, it had the sound of a school punishment for a boy who never really grew up. A week later, after George had apologised and promised to mend his ways (where have we heard that before?), he was reinstated and, if it's not a contradiction in terms, promptly missed training.

He was sacked on the same day as Frank O'Farrell but claimed to have quit the club before his own dismissal and, at the age of 26, added, 'I will never play for Manchester United again. I am finished with the game.'

Matt was unequivocal in his public response. 'All of us on the board were at the end of our tether,' he said. 'We'd had enough of George and his nightclubs and his way of life.'

That was where Tommy came in – left in the invidious position of having one of the greatest players who ever lived still contracted to his desperately struggling club, and he couldn't even select him.

After paying Arsenal £120,000 for George Graham (one of the infamous 10-pin bowlers from days gone by) and being knocked out of the FA Cup 1–0 at Wolves in the third round, TD's next step was to persuade an understandably hesitant Matt that he, the new manager, could tame the unmanageable. TD then spent countless hours of his personal time preying on their shared love of the game to persuade United's most prized asset to wear the famous red shirt again – even to the point of promising Best that he didn't even have to turn up on time and train like other mere mortals. Not ideal for team morale, perhaps, but I'm sure that it must have appealed to the wayward Irish genius.

With Denis, the situation could not have been more different. Tommy quickly found Law's influence within the club unacceptable and didn't like the cliques that seemed to exist around every murmuring corner. It was clear, at least to me, that Denis's days were numbered. On Friday, 27 April 1973, United were just about to travel to Chelsea for their last game of the season and the end of Bobby Charlton's distinguished playing career, when Tommy called Law into his office after training and told him that he was effectively calling time on his Manchester United career. He was giving him a free transfer. As if this wasn't enough, the next step in his treatment of Denis was completely indefensible.

A naturally dumbfounded Denis was due a testimonial against Ajax at the start of the following season and suggested – half-pleaded I would imagine – that he could use that occasion to announce his retirement. It would allow him the kind of dignified exit that his service to the club undeniably deserved. It would also spare Denis's family any undue stress at what was a traumatic time for them: Law's mother was being treated for cancer, his wife, Di, was five months pregnant and they were just about to move into a new house. TD happily agreed to delay the announcement of Denis's departure and Law immediately drove up to Scotland to collect his children at the end of their Easter holiday.

In a pub in Aberdeen the following lunchtime, Denis was trying to enjoy a quiet drink with some friends when his picture appeared on the television screen accompanied by the news that United had given him a free transfer. I would read of Law's anger later and could only sympathise. When he arrived home from London, I told Tommy it was an unforgivable thing to have done but he just shrugged and said that it had 'slipped out' when he was talking to some reporters. I honestly have no idea, but I imagine that if Docherty and Law have ever spoken a word to one another since it can only have been a threatening one.

Partially based on that suspicion, my son Tom was quite apprehensive some 20 years later when he was asked to produce the United documentary that I referred to several chapters ago. He would be working with some of his heroes but, not for the first time in his life, he was also painfully aware that his name might make the situation awkward, if not untenable. He needn't have worried. When that European Cup-winning team were obviously informed of Tom's family background and, far more pertinently, of the fact that he hadn't spoken to his father since the summer of 1977, they all treated him as if he had been an unused substitute on the bench the night they won it. In fact, he rang after he had finished filming to tell me that every single one of them had been fantastic – and by far and away the most helpful of all had been Denis Law.

Although they lost 1–0 at Stamford Bridge in Bobby Charlton's farewell appearance to a goal by one of Tommy's protégés, Peter Osgood, my husband's renowned motivational skills had somehow enabled United to escape relegation by the comparatively comfortable margin of seven points. But the decay was so deep-rooted that Tommy had only succeeded in postponing the inevitable, especially without the mercurial skills of Best. Despite the United manager continuing to whisper sweet nothings into his ear at regular intervals, the only game George was playing was hard to get.

Meanwhile, the Lawman, as so many supporters called him, joined Manchester City that summer. An ageing gunslinger in search of one last showdown. But how could any of us have possibly known that the fates were conspiring to play such a trick?

If revenge is a dish best served cold, then Denis must have kept Tommy's dinner in the deep freezer for 12 months. In his impatience to overhaul the club, the United manager may have thought that Law was way past his sell-by date but, on 27 April 1974, exactly a year to the day since TD had told one of the greatest strikers who ever loitered with lethal intent inside a penalty area that his services were no longer required, Denis came back to haunt the Theatre of Dreams...

Above: Peter shoots while Michael signs as a professional footballer for Burnley in November 1967. Harry Potts, the former manager of Burnley is pictured with us.

Below left: The start of our nomadic life, post-Chelsea – perhaps I shouldn't have bothered unpacking ...

Below right: A present for my 40th birthday – a portrait of my four beautiful children.

Above: What a goal! Back home from Oporto for the summer.

Below: Birdbaths for goalposts! Peter puts one past his dad. For the first time in his career, in 1971, Tommy was out of a job.

Our silver wedding anniversary party at the Playboy Club in Manchester. Among the guests were members of our family, Sir Matt Busby (with me, middle left) and Paddy Crerand (pictured top, second from the left).

Above: From the Gorbals of Glasgow to the Vatican. *From left to right*: Sir Matt Busby, Louis Edwards, the Chairman of Utd at the time, Bobby Charlton in the final year of his playing career, and Tommy, meet Pope Paul VI.

Below: A dejected-looking Tommy after Manchester United were relegated to the old Second Division. They lost 1–0 to Manchester City and, ironically, Denis Law scored the vital goal for the winning team.

Tommy giving away our beautiful daughter, Catherine, on Sunday
26th January, 1975.

Installed in the home of my dreams with the man of my dreams – Tommy and I at our house in Manchester in 1976.

What a difference a year makes. *Above left*: 1976, the year Manchester Utd lost to Southampton – I had to coax Tommy onto the dancefloor with me. *Above right*: A year on in 1977, and we beat Liverpool 2–1 to win the FA Cup. Tommy is pictured here with Peter.

Below: After seven failed attempts as player and manager, Tommy finally triumphs at Wembley.

Above: FA Cup celebration dinner. Mrs Brown is identified on the table behind ours. Notice my husband's body language!

Below: With my son, Tom, and his daughter, my adorable granddaughter Amy, all dressed up for her role in *Annie*. It was my wonderful family who helped me through the pain of my separation from Tommy.

CHAPTER 12

GLORY GLORY MAN UNITED?

Man's love is of man's life a thing apart,
'Tis woman's whole existence.
LORD BYRON (1788–1824)

I have read and heard it said so many times that today it's almost a cliché but, once asked to summarise his team's performance, Tommy was the first person that I'm actually aware of using the phrase: 'We started badly – and fell away.'

I can't recall exactly when it was but had he been describing United's entire 1973/74 season it would have been an accurate assessment. In fact, that disastrous campaign was only a couple of months old when Matt Busby phoned one rainy Monday evening to ask if he could drop round for an hour or so.

We had lost 1–0 at home to Derby County the previous Saturday to lie 18th in the table with just eight points from the opening 11 games. It was our third defeat in a row. Even so, I still assumed that Matt was just coming round for a chat. He was too much of a gentleman to exclude me from the conversation so, on Matt's polite insistence, I sat but merely listened as he gently reassured my husband that, if we should happen to be relegated, it wouldn't matter in the slightest. 'Don't worry,' he said in that familiar brogue that so reminded me of another Matt, my dear dad. 'It wouldn't be the end of the world – just part of the rebuilding process.'

At that, he smiled at each of us in turn and I could swear I saw in his eyes that, for his own unspoken reasons and all the way back to a snowbound runway in Munich, he held himself partially responsible for the club's current demise. Nobody knew more about rebuilding than that man, but long after he had left I honestly wasn't too sure that my husband either understood the purpose of the visit or appreciated it. I knew that I did.

I also strongly suspected there was another reason for Matt's unexpected call. Despite the frequent rumours that he was prone to interfere from the moment he ceased to be the manager, in our experience Matt never once meddled in team matters and was quite happy to let TD get on with it. However, a certain player had finally succumbed to my husband's advances and been back in training for several weeks. So, on this occasion and like everybody else following the feverish media speculation, Matt simply wanted to know if the prodigal son was ready to return to action. Tommy had been delighted to confirm that, yes, George Best would indeed be starting against Birmingham City at Old Trafford the following Saturday.

Despite George's admittedly rather rusty return to action, the game was won by a more unlikely source – United goalkeeper Alex Stepney, who scored a penalty in a narrow 1–0 win. This actually made Stepney joint top scorer on two goals with Brian Kidd and Sammy McIlroy. Such was the fragility that flowed through the team they were clearly more than happy to leave the responsibility of spot-kicks to the keeper. 'If I played like I did today every week,' Best later told a small army of journalists, 'I would worry about staying in the team.'

He had every reason to worry. Tommy's lengthy seduction technique may have centred around the promise that George didn't need to concern himself with such mundane matters as training and punctuality, but the famous philanderer had made the mistake of taking the manager at his word. As the weeks slipped by, his fitness and performances on the pitch barely improved. When we lost 2–0 at Liverpool in the last match before Christmas, to languish in 19th place with 14 points from 20 games, I could tell that Doctor Jekyll was rapidly losing patience.

After yet another defeat, 3–0 at QPR on Tuesday, 1 January 1974, it was apparent that Tommy's only New Year resolution was the permanent removal of another Old Trafford legend. Whether the opportunity presented itself or was completely fabricated will always be a matter of conjecture between the two individuals concerned. Either way, the inevitable outcome was another example of TD's ruthless streak, one of the perceived attributes, don't forget, that had prompted the directors to employ him in the first place.

The manager's version of events on the following Saturday for the FA Cup third-round tie at home to Third Division Plymouth Argyle was that the player turned up drunk, compulsory blonde in tow and 10 minutes before kick-off.

'What was I supposed to do?' Tommy asked me when he returned home that night after the 1–0 win. 'Let him play?'

George later responded by telling reporters, 'I wouldn't have insulted the team nor the fans in that way. He had to find an excuse so he went ahead and made one up. That was it for me. I didn't even watch the game I was so insulted.'

Best was 27 years old and never played for Manchester United again.

After we were knocked out of the Cup 1–0 at home by Ipswich Town in the following round, the season started to spiral out of control. Towards the end of April, we were waking up every morning and staring the spectre of relegation in the face, but I would constantly reassure myself by recalling and trusting a promise made to *both* of us that everything would be fine, that it was all 'just part of the rebuilding process'.

I have already mentioned the depth of decay that existed at United when Tommy accepted that job. Yet even the most imaginative scriptwriter would have been forced to dismiss the following sequence of events as far too implausible to place before an audience. That the back-heeled death blow after 82 minutes – the only goal of the game and the one that ultimately condemned United to the Second Division – would be administered in front of a full house of almost 57,000 people at Old Trafford by Denis Law. Scoring what turned out to be the final goal of his career for, of all teams, Manchester City.

Glancing down in my own despair towards him, I could tell that my husband was most definitely numb. The controversial goalscorer was immediately substituted and the newspapers would speculate that Law was so upset at applying the *coup de grace* to his old team that he was simply unable to continue. Stone-faced, he hadn't even celebrated the goal with his trademark stiff-armed salute. Maybe, but my own theory is that, as much as he undoubtedly loved that club, Denis was removed from the predictable mayhem to prevent him from looking over at the United manager and then laughing and sticking two fingers up at him.

The terrace fire and pitch invasion that followed, with City players being kicked, punched and spat upon as they fled for safety from thousands of desperate United fans attempting to get the game abandoned, only served to magnify to me how far this once great club had plummeted. It was a miracle that nobody was seriously injured or worse. Advised by the police that it was unsafe to continue and that returning to the pitch would only inflame the situation, referee David Smith officially abandoned the game after 86 minutes, but the score was later and quite rightly allowed to stand.

Sporting history records it as the first season that the Football League introduced the three-up, three-down system. It would also do well to remember that amid cries in the papers for various punishments such as a hefty fine, future ground closure and that 'these animals should be caged!' United went down in disgrace in 21st place, while Southampton and Norwich City were relegated with relative dignity.

Tommy was never one to dwell and perhaps that was just as well. He had a serious rebuilding job to continue and, probing for positives, he reasoned that the relatively less stressful Second Division was just the place to do it. The spotlight in the lower tier of English football was equally bright purely because this was Manchester United but the opposition, if not the audience, was slightly less demanding. Instead of forthcoming fixtures against Liverpool and Newcastle, I now found myself writing the likes of Leyton Orient and Notts County on my calendars.

After all, he had taken Chelsea straight back up to the top flight a dozen years before and, as he retained the experience of Alex Stepney in goal, Martin Buchan in defence and Willie Morgan on the wing, he swiftly assembled a vibrant young side around them. And, in the same way as I stated before about his early days at Stamford Bridge, any self-respecting United fan can still reverently recite the names of Gordon Hill, Steve Coppell, Brian Greenhoff, Gerry Daly, Lou Macari and Stuart Pearson as members of one of the most exciting teams that even that great club ever possessed.

'Number two son' as I often referred to him, left home that summer to live in the Cheshire countryside with two friends about 30 miles away and start his working life as a trainee journalist on the Warrington Guardian Series. But not before unwittingly providing me with an insight into growing up as the child of a father who occasionally occupied more column inches in the national newspapers than the Prime Minister.

Several days after my son's interview, I answered the phone to somebody asking if they could speak to 'Tom Johnson'. When I questioned the name, Tom took the receiver and, having been offered one of only six posts from over 300 applicants, he thanked the caller before explaining that he had given a false name. As I listened, he said, 'I'm very sorry, but I never wanted to think that you've only given me the job because of who my father is.'

Halfway through the 1974/75 season, as United stormed back into the First Division at the first time of asking, I was anxious to arrange a very important party for Friday, 27 December. As United were away to Oldham Athletic the following day I had to concede defeat and delay the occasion until the Saturday evening. I couldn't be annoyed because it seemed somehow apposite that, 25 years after being forced to move our wedding back a day, football should once again take precedence over my plans. When I asked Tommy several weeks earlier where he thought we should hold the event, his blank expression – certainly for the sake of his immediate health! – lifted only just in time. I was, after all, discussing our silver wedding anniversary.

I would have much preferred a fairly small restaurant with just our nearest and dearest, but he decided that it should be at the Playboy Club, a regular haunt of some of his own new 'friends' that I preferred to think of as hangers-on. He also insisted that the extensive guest list of well over 100 include at least a dozen people I had never met in my life. However, in my determination to enjoy our marital milestone, I acquiesced and sent out the invitations.

The centre of attention, where he always loved to be, surrounded by every person in his life that I thought he held dear, my husband looked like he wished he could be somewhere else. Rarely smiling, declining to dance, refusing to make even the shortest speech and drinking just two glasses of champagne throughout the entire evening, Tommy's subdued mood perplexed me. I can fully understand anybody being briefly reflective at such a moment in their lives – after all, a quarter of a century is a long time to be married and I had several such pauses myself that night – but my husband seemed to be reluctantly acknowledging the occasion rather than actually celebrating it.

United had lost 1–0 at Oldham, only their fourth defeat in 25 games that season, but they were still four points clear at the top of the table and I wasn't prepared to attribute his sullen behaviour to that afternoon's result. I decided to put it down to the pressure of his profession and, although United were knocked out of the FA Cup the following week 3–2 in a third-round replay by Third Division Walsall, TD wasn't too perturbed as he thought it would enable the team to concentrate on the priority of promotion.

We were confirmed as Second Division champions on Saturday, 5 April 1975, by winning 1–0 at Southampton. There were still three games remaining but the victory, with a goal from Lou Macari, left us seven points clear of our nearest challengers, Sunderland. Nor was the irony lost on me that Chelsea moved in the opposite direction that particular season. I was so happy that, after checking with Peter and Tom, who was home for the weekend, I brazenly decided to ignore those countless changes of plan, postponements and cancellations that the world of football had always dictated down the years and hold an impromptu party. Firstly, I phoned the Busby family then, dependent at such short notice on the geography of where they lived, close friends and various other usual suspects, until I discovered that we had no fewer than 27 instant guests!

Our large lounge was towards the back of the house with French windows and steps leading down to the swimming pool and I asked a tired but very excited Peter to sit in darkness in the front room and keep an eye out for his dad coming home. It was almost midnight when my youngest son ran in to tell me that the car had just pulled into the driveway. We turned all the lights off and stood in complete silence, champagne in hand and hearts in mouths as Tommy opened the door, stumbled down the hallway and into the lounge in search of an invisible switch and muttered, 'That's bloody great. We've just been promoted and they've all gone to bed!' He nearly jumped out of his skin when I turned the lights back on and the packed room erupted in a mixture of laughter and applause.

By the time that party finally ended over nine hours later, I was fast running out of rashers and laughing even more at the unlikely sight of Matt through the kitchen window. After all, it's not every day that you see a barefooted knight of the realm with the trousers of his immaculate suit rolled up to the knees, dangling his feet in the shallow end of your pool and happily munching a bacon sandwich. He laughed and declined my offer of a knotted hankie to protect his head from the bright sunlight. How could I have imagined that one day Tommy would walk and then self-destruct in such a great man's shadow?

Returning his plate about 10 minutes later, Matt found me alone and asked if he could have a quiet word. 'I'm proud of Tommy,' he said, 'and the team he has created. They're a credit to the club's tradition but he couldn't have done any of it without you. I know – because you remind me of a young Jean.'

I have remembered every single one of those words simply because I'm not sure I ever received a greater compliment.

To come straight back up and finish third behind QPR and only four points behind the champions, Liverpool, at the end of the 1975/76 season was quite an achievement in itself. To find ourselves back on the Wembley trail only added to the considerable excitement. I didn't dare to dream of returning to the old place until we were drawn to face Derby County in the semi-final at Hillsborough. I couldn't even bring myself to go to the game and, not for the first time, resorted to the radio. I shouldn't have worried. A 2–0 United victory, courtesy of two Gordon Hill goals, meant that we were back in the Cup Final. I was also convinced that our time had finally come.

Once as a player for Preston, four times as an international for Scotland and once as the manager of Chelsea, Tommy had left that stadium with only a 2–2 draw against England on his first appearance there as any tangible reward. Now, on Saturday, 1 May 1976, a vibrant, young Manchester United would be playing the veterans of Second Division Southampton. I knew it would be seventh time lucky for my husband. I wasn't being arrogant. I just knew that we couldn't possibly lose.

It was offside. Anybody could see that – except Clive Thomas and, unfortunately for us, he happened to be the man in black on that spring afternoon. So, when the late Bobby Stokes's 82nd-minute shot was allowed to stand, it created one of the greatest FA Cup Final upsets of all time. Second time unlucky as a manager and yet two completely unrelated thoughts occurred to me as I stood and slowly shook my head at the final whistle. The solitary goal was scored in the same minute of the match as Law's retribution two seasons earlier, and the Cup Final referee was from Treorchy, a town midway between Pontypridd and Swansea. I couldn't help but wonder if he was aware of Tommy's hatred of the Welsh!

Despite the result, we actually had such a terrific time afterwards it was as though we'd won the trophy. Once again, I had been unwittingly cast in the role of matriarch, so that when Tommy arrived back at our suite at the Royal Lancaster Hotel it was packed with sympathetic friends and visitors. Although he was charming to everybody, I instantly recognised the look he gave me from across the room and over the top of his dry white wine glass half an hour later. So I started to politely herd them all out by suggesting it was time to get changed for the evening function. Then, as TD soaked in the bath, I perched on the side and we talked about the match. He was remarkably philosophical about losing yet again to the point where I found myself thinking of the young man who had furiously thrown his loser's medal against the wall of another hotel in London 22 years earlier.

That recollection also caused me to briefly contemplate the fact that the closest we had ever come to spending any quality time with that elusive piece of silverware was when it spent the weekend as an unwelcome guest in our house. Tommy's attitude was that some people never get *one* shot at it so we should be grateful. I was impressed. Surprised to hear it coming from a man who despised defeat so much, but impressed nevertheless.

We duly attended the dinner and Tommy gave a wonderfully witty and impromptu speech, praised his own team and the opposition and then performed his party piece. It was an acceptable rendition of an old Sinatra song and the players all held up the reservation numbers on their tables as if they were awarding him points.

As I listened to and joined the laughter that masked the disappointment in that room, I had no reason to suspect that it was probably the last night my husband wanted me anywhere in his life.

My wonderful wee aunt Helen, my mum's sister, died the following week, leaving me feeling guilty of the charge of caring about a game of football. I drove alone to the funeral in Motherwell on Tuesday, 11 May, as Tommy was already in nearby Glasgow for the European Cup Final between Bayern Munich and St Etienne the next night. He joined me for the Requiem Mass but was so cold and distant that I found myself wishing he really hadn't bothered. I was already very distressed at losing my dear aunt, but Tommy had loved her, too, which made his attitude all the more baffling.

Aunt Helen and Uncle Mick used to travel down to stay with us for a fortnight every summer regardless of where we were living and, on the first morning, she would ritually remove all the curtains in the house and wash them! My spinal problem prevented me from carrying out the task but, even if I had been able or paid for somebody else to, I always 'saved' the chore for her, secretly smiling in the knowledge that she liked to think she was earning her keep.

Similarly, at some point during their stay, she would inevitably turn to Tommy and say, 'You know, you're such a lucky man to have our Agnes.' Whether that was true or not, Uncle Mick needed no reminding of his own good fortune in being married to such a woman. In fact, he only lived a matter of months beyond the death of his beloved wife.

She was more than everything to him and, after Tommy, he was one of the funniest men I ever knew. Our children always called them aunt and uncle too and loved it when they came to stay. I remember Tom, when he was about eight and we were living in London, running into their bedroom to wake them up one morning and being fascinated by the fact that his great-uncle was lying there fast asleep – wearing his glasses. He urgently shook him awake and asked, 'Uncle Mick, why are you sleeping with your glasses on?'

He turned to look at this inquisitive wee boy staring at him from roughly 18 inches away and said, 'So I can see what I'm dreaming.'

Tommy drove straight back to Glasgow after the funeral and was robbed that night in his hotel room of £600 in cash and his glasses. Maybe he should have worn them in his sleep. He has always been extremely short-sighted but he hated to wear his 'bins', as he called them, in public – even to the extent of driving without them. I don't believe it was a case of vanity. I think he considered his myopia to be some sign of weakness. As always, I dealt with the insurance claim and the subsequent correspondence which included an indignant letter from the hotel manager. He had written to tell me that Tommy's room door had not been forced and resented the subsequent suspicion that had been cast on his 'trustworthy staff'.

Ten days later, on 22 May, and with virtually the entire

world to choose from, United had arranged a trip to Bermuda. It was more of an end-of-season tour than a pre-season one, but I found it hard to believe that Tommy was returning to that country. I wasn't even sure they would let him in after the debacle there nine years before. We had privately arranged at our own expense that Tommy would stay on after the tour ended on 9 June and I would fly out the same day. A taxi was picking me up at 10:30 am to take me to Manchester Airport for the first leg of my journey and I was so excited at the prospect of a week in such an exotic place. TD had apparently met the Governor of Bermuda who, on learning that he was to extend his trip and was being joined by me, promptly sent an official invitation for us to attend Government House as his guests on 14 June for a dinner party to celebrate Her Majesty The Queen's official birthday.

As I was sitting in my dressing gown at the breakfast table with Peter, happily fretting about my outfit for the function, the telephone rang and made me jump. It was 8:00 am and, after accepting the charge for the long distance call, I listened as Tommy told me that he was on his way back to England. It didn't make any sense. The time difference meant that it was 4:00 am in Bermuda but he wasn't prepared to offer any explanation. What was he doing in the departure area in the middle of their night? At first I was speechless and, after putting the receiver down, I became angry and confused. But what argument could I possibly have offered in a short transatlantic call to make him stay there when he was obviously so determined to come home?

I even briefly considered the possibility that, now he was no longer travelling under the umbrella of the official Manchester United touring party, he was being deported as an 'undesirable'. I certainly had no desire to see him when he eventually arrived home and never did discover the reason. His erratic behaviour should have served as a warning to me, but not for the first time I refused to believe he could ever treat me so thoughtlessly again. In less than a month, I would be proved completely wrong.

It may only have been the UEFA Cup, but United's third-place finish in the previous campaign meant they were back in Europe for the first time in seven frustrating seasons. Far too long for a club of that stature. The draw for the first round was to be made in Zurich on Monday, 5 July, and the club secretary, Les Olive, suggested to Tommy that they should take their wives on the trip. The club was funding the cost of their work-related journey and our husbands would each naturally pay for Betty and I to accompany them. Don't ask me how a draw lasting less than an hour necessitates a week at a luxury hotel in Lausanne but I certainly wasn't about to complain. Switzerland had been a dream location of mine for many years, fuelled in part by the fact that Tommy had stayed there for the 1954 World Cup and enjoyed it so much, even if Scotland's visit had been predictably brief.

As we checked into our beautiful hotel, we were initially puzzled to discover that it was packed to the rafters with immaculately dressed Americans. Betty and I quickly realised the reason but, throughout the delicious buffet, dancing and subsequently spectacular firework display that was almost drowned out by the whooping and hollering of our fellow guests, our partners still didn't make the connection.

Not only was it the Fourth of July, it was also the bicentennial of American Independence Day. They had 200 years to celebrate in a single night and weren't prepared to waste a moment. I knew precisely how they felt because I was finally allowed to dance until the music stopped. That was at 3:00 am and, from my hometown beach in Girvan to the shores of Lake Geneva in a comparatively mere 27 years, I felt I had plenty to celebrate too.

The following morning, Les and Tommy travelled back into Zurich where United were given a difficult draw against Ajax of Amsterdam. Betty and I took the opportunity to go shopping. Or perhaps that should be staring, the prices being what they were. Not surprisingly, we returned to the hotel empty-handed and went in search of our respective husbands. Having firstly tried the room, I found mine sitting glum-faced and alone in the lounge. Without even saying hello, he told me that he was going home the following morning.

I was dumbfounded but he said he had promised to attend the university graduation of the United right-winger Steve Coppell. I was aware that occasion was imminent but I was also convinced Tommy had delegated the appointment. I stressed that he was being stupid by breaking his holiday because, in spite of the UEFA Cup draw, that's precisely what it was. Steve would be the first to understand. But, oh no, out of the blue he was going home and mentioned that he had already rearranged his flight. Surely he meant *our* flights? No, he said, I would be staying there for the rest of the week with Les and Betty.

I didn't want the Olives to feel they had to include me in their plans but, on being told the news by Tommy over a drink later that evening, they encouraged me to stay on with them. I was hesitant but began to think that maybe I should – if only because of my husband's hostile manner towards me. Les and Betty knew me well enough to sense my awkwardness but they were extremely kind and took me on several trips to the surrounding lakes and mountains. At other times, I would feign tiredness and sit alone with my book in the hotel gardens but I found it difficult to read. My concentration kept wandering and I often felt frightened by the uncertainty of the future.

Much later, of course, I learned that was the week that Catherine first became suspicious of her father. She was at home looking after Peter and apparently upon his premature return Tommy was out every night until the early hours. He told her he was attending various functions but she knew from his casual attire that he was lying and even checked the mileage on his car every morning to compare it to where he claimed to have been the previous evening.

My daughter is more like her father in so many ways than our sons are. I mean no disrespect by that but she has an awareness, a shrewdness that the boys don't possess. Clocking the distance he had driven would simply never have crossed their minds. And anyway, TD was even brazen enough to give her a clue regarding his behaviour when she asked him to have dinner at home one evening. He said that he couldn't, smiled on his way out of the door and added, 'When the cat's away...!'

Apart from sleeping, it seemed the longest period of time he spent at the house in my absence was one afternoon when Laurie Brown and his wife and children happened to turn up with their swimming costumes and stayed for several hours. Catherine remembered noticing a complete change in her father's demeanour. Then she realised what it was – and it made her feel sick. She was watching her middle-aged father flirting like a love-struck teenager. I flew home from Zurich on the Sunday afternoon and, again much later as she didn't want to upset me, my daughter told me she'd had to plead with Tommy to collect me from the airport.

I may have been scared but I didn't share Catherine's private suspicions during that gloriously long, hot summer of 1976. It never occurred to me to check up on him. His working hours had always been erratic but now it was becoming impossible to predict his changes of mood. It wasn't quite treading on eggshells, but I did feel that a degree of delicacy was frequently required and that was when I began to wonder if everything was okay at Old Trafford. I was genuinely worried about his health and could only hope that whatever was troubling him would pass. We would sometimes sit in bed and talk at length – there was a time when those conversations had taken place once a night, now it was about once a fortnight.

Although I had learned long ago not to ask too many questions or dig too deeply, I could always tell when I had scratched the surface of the truth. He would automatically go on the defensive and utter the two words that, as far as he was concerned, signalled the abrupt end to any conversation that he felt was becoming too uncomfortable to continue: 'Behave yourself.'

The rest of that year served only as an unwelcome prelude to the nightmare of 1977. No matter the time of night, I always waited up to meet Tommy at the front door when I heard his car, but my welcome-home hug and kiss were not only no longer reciprocated, they were more often than not brushed aside. There was no lipstick on the collar but he would nervously avoid any eye contact and there was an inflection in his voice that suggested an underlying distress that he was either unwilling or unable to discuss.

I wanted so much to ease his obvious suffering but how could I help when he wouldn't share it with me? I hoped it was simply tiredness and sometimes I think it genuinely was. He had always worked very hard but now I realise that living such a deceitful life must have been a tremendous burden. I started going to bed at around midnight and would read until whatever time he came home. If he didn't come straight upstairs, I would go down and see if he wanted a snack, such as his favourite bacon sandwich, but he would invariably say he had already eaten.

Another part of Tommy also changed when the executive suite and grill room opened at Old Trafford the previous season. He would often have both his lunch and dinner there – surrounded by the people he called friends. I knew nearly all of them by now and preferred to think of them as sycophants. Our sparse and valuable time at home together suffered as a result and I would jokingly ask him if my cooking was so bad that he needed to dine there all the time.

One night that winter, I was watching the evening news in bed while Tommy stared intently at the league table in the newspaper. I could almost hear his thoughts: 'If *we* win tomorrow and *they* lose and *they* only draw then we'll be second!'

I broke the spell by saying, 'I wonder if the Browns' marriage is in trouble.'

Tommy casually asked why I thought that and I told him Mrs Brown had mentioned to one of the less discreet wives at the club that she had been out to dinner several times with a prominent local businessman and was becoming very fond of him.

Without looking up, Tommy sniggered and said, 'If that's true, then, whoever he is, he must be bloody desperate!'

CHAPTER 13

SECRETS AND LIES

*The worst sin towards our fellow creatures is not
to hate them,
but to be indifferent to them: that's the essence of inhumanity.*

George Bernard Shaw (1856–1950)

1977. It was to be quite a year. Maybe you remember it for the Silver Jubilee, the golden summer that Virginia Wade won Wimbledon, Red Rum romping home in the Grand National for the third and final time, Jimmy Carter being elected President – or simply the year that Elvis died. I would much rather forget it altogether.

After beating QPR 1–0 at Old Trafford in the fourth round of the FA Cup at the end of January, Tommy came home and asked me to make an appointment with our solicitor to discuss our last will and testaments and to review our various insurance policies and pension plans. It was completely out of character. He always shuddered and stopped me in mid-sentence when I so much as started an 'if anything should ever happen to us...' conversation. Now here he was suddenly suggesting that we should evaluate our financial affairs.

After amending our wills slightly, examining the existing policies and thanking our solicitor, we were walking back to the car when Tommy turned to me with tears in his eyes and said, 'It's all yours then.'

It was so disconcerting that I was unable to reply. Then, when the draft documents arrived in the post, he refused to sign them anyway. I can only assume that in between the visit to the solicitor and the arrival of the documents an unknown (to me) third party had insisted that Tommy shouldn't be so hasty.

Yet it wasn't constant despondency. On my 48th birthday, Tommy told me he had a surprise and asked me to meet him at Old Trafford. From there, he whisked me off to the home of Harold Riley, the world-renowned artist. Harold is Salford born and bred and a United fanatic, and we had known him socially since first arriving in Manchester. He greeted us at the door and asked us to wait in the lounge. Looking at the works of homegrown art on the walls, my attention was caught by a portrait resting on an easel in the corner. It was a schoolboy in uniform. 'Tommy! That looks *just* like our Peter!' I said.

At that moment, Harold came back into the room, accompanied by his gorgeous and heavily pregnant wife, Ashraf, a bottle of champagne and four crystal glasses. He toasted my health, pointed at the painting in the corner of the room, smiled and said, 'Do you like your present, Agnes?'

It *was* Peter! I don't think I have ever received a gift in my entire life that gave me so much pleasure. It seemed Harold had wanted to paint a portrait of my husband for me but Tommy had suggested our youngest son should be the subject instead. It was definitely one of his better decisions that year.

Tommy could be his old self at other times, too, and never more than when the family occasionally gathered en masse for Sunday lunch. He loved to play the role of the patriarch and, when our children and grandchildren were leaving, he would walk on to the road and literally stop the traffic with a wave of his hand while they reversed out of the drive. Then he would pretend to exhaustedly stagger back into the house as if the entire day had all been too much for him, flop into his favourite chair and we would happily reflect on the success our three eldest children were making of their lives. If I could rewind my life, one of the places I'd stop the tape would be at such an afternoon. They were delightful days.

As that season travelled towards its dramatic conclusion in more ways than one, I tried to behave like a normal wife while constantly wondering what was happening to my husband. He appeared to be fighting demons. Twice in the space of one week in the middle of March, I asked him if there was another woman and he emphatically denied it. I remember saying to him one night, 'Listen, darling, if you are having problems at United, then just pack it in. There will be a queue for your services outside the door first thing tomorrow morning.'

One Monday morning I received a call from a young lady called Lavinia Warner at London Weekend Television. She was a researcher for *This Is Your Life* and told me that they had Tommy in mind as one of their upcoming 'victims'. I didn't say so at the time, but I was initially hesitant to co-operate because of Tommy's current erratic behaviour and mood swings. I told her I'd call her back later that week and, after consulting an enthusiastic Matt Busby and United chairman, Louis Edwards, decided to go with it. I thought it might even somehow bring my husband to his senses.

Never one for shunning the limelight, I thought Tommy would relish an evening of back-slapping, surrounded by his family and friends. I spent quite a few hours in clandestine meetings and conversations with Lavinia (unaware that my husband was dealing in his own particular brand of subterfuge at the same time) and provided her with information, anecdotes and old family photographs. However, as events unfolded over the next few weeks, the show was just one of the many casualties of my marital breakdown.

Around that time, United beat Leeds 2–1 in the FA Cup semi-final and, once again, the dream of Wembley and Tommy's final fulfilment at the eighth time of asking was on the horizon. But something else was on the horizon, too – the beginning of my personal nightmare.

Ronnie Corbett, a dear friend going back almost 20 years to our Arsenal days, was performing in cabaret at a nearby nightclub for a fortnight and we had arranged to go to United's home game against QPR on 30 April. As we were having lunch and laughing at shared memories in the executive suite prior to the match (which we won 1–0), Tommy came in to say hello to wee Ronnie. He ignored me completely and my guest couldn't have failed to notice.

When TD left about 10 minutes later, Ronnie looked anxiously at me and asked, 'How is he, Agnes?'

I pretended everything was fine but Ronnie is a wonderful comic actor and I don't think he was fooled by my amateur, arm-waving dramatics for a single moment. He wrote me such a kind letter after Tommy left home, offering to help *both* of us and suggesting we should use his holiday cottage as 'a hideaway'. Typical of the man.

On the Monday evening, 2 May, Tommy attended the Scottish Sports Writers' Association's annual dinner in Glasgow. I understood he was staying in the city overnight until the 8:00 am radio news on Tuesday morning reported he had been involved in a car accident on the A74 near Dumfries. I was horrified and immediately rang his sister, Margaret, in Glasgow. Her husband, Stuart, answered and said they too had just heard the bulletin. He explained that Tommy had been at their house before suddenly deciding to drive back to Manchester at 1:30 am. They had tried to dissuade him but he was insistent.

Apparently, an articulated lorry had jack-knifed into his path. Tommy's Mercedes was a write-off. It was a miracle, the police told me, he hadn't been killed and that it was only from the discovery of various documents in the wreckage of the car that they had been able to ascertain the identity of the driver. A driver who had now disappeared. I rang United and spoke to the lovely Kath on the switchboard. Everyone at the club was extremely worried, she told me, but, no, they hadn't seen him and didn't know where he might be. I paced around the kitchen like a caged animal, frightened to use the phone again in case Tommy or anybody else was trying to contact me.

Then, at 12:45 pm, Kath phoned and said she had just seen

him getting out of a taxi on the Old Trafford forecourt and he appeared to be perfectly all right. 'Thank God,' I remember saying before asking her to get him to call me immediately. He rang at just after 2:00 pm and sounded almost blasé about the entire episode, telling me that he had hitched a lift back to the outskirts of Manchester with a United-mad lorry driver. I was so relieved to know he was safe that his total disregard for the people who had been so concerned about him supplanted my annoyance. That thoughtless attitude was further emphasised when I read a newspaper story a couple of weeks later reporting that he had promised the lorry driver two tickets for the Cup Final and the man was complaining that he hadn't received them.

On Wednesday, 4 May, Tommy arrived home at 1:45 am in very high spirits. I was still awake, sitting up in bed reading, when he burst into the bedroom clutching a bottle of champagne which, without the aid of a glass, he proceeded to single-handedly empty in the space of about 30 minutes. He told me how wonderful I was and that we were celebrating his new, improved contract with United – to be signed later – and insisted that in spite of the late hour I phone our eldest son, Michael, to tell him the news. I was finding it increasingly difficult to cope with this Jekyll and Hyde character, a man capable of complete detachment followed by a flood of flowers and affection.

Then, if it was at all possible, my state of perpetual anxiety intensified five days later when I answered the door to discover two police officers asking if could they please speak to my husband.

Inviting them in, I apologised by explaining that he had

already left for work. After offering them a cup of tea and asking if he had been caught speeding again, I enquired if I could help in any way. The male officer smiled awkwardly and told me they had received a complaint from an 11-year-old boy's mother claiming Tommy had assaulted her son outside the public phone box in the village square the previous evening. The boy had subsequently spent the night in hospital under observation. I could hardly believe my ears! It seemed that the boy had asked for Tommy's autograph and he had refused. The young policeman then blushed slightly as he added, 'I'm afraid this is where it becomes a little bit delicate.' He told me there had been mention of another woman.

According to his statement, the boy had said to Tommy that, if he didn't give him an autograph, he would 'tell your wife about your fancy woman'. It was alleged that Tommy had then slapped the child across the side of the face. I refused to accept a word of it. For a start, I thought, why on earth would my husband be using a public phone about a quarter of a mile from our house? Furthermore, in my experience Tommy rarely, if ever, refused to grant a request for an autograph. The police thanked me for the tea and said they would drive to Old Trafford to interview Tommy.

When he returned that evening, TD said that he had given a statement strenuously denying any accusation of assault. He told me the boy had been 'messing about' with his car while he was on the phone and he had merely told him off.

So I asked, 'But why were you using that phone at all when you were so close to home?'

He told me a story about how he had forgotten to call his

sister, Margaret, who had asked to borrow some money. I was suspicious. Why hadn't he waited to get home before ringing her? Repeating the remarks the boy had made to the police about a 'fancy woman', I insisted he should tell me more.

Tommy glared at me and quietly hissed, 'Behave yourself.'

In the end, the incident quietly went away. I don't recall the exact circumstances. What I do remember is that the next morning I had to endure a visit from the boy's mother and elder sister, who came to my house and called my husband all the names under the sun as I stood and listened to them on my doorstep in the rain.

When the two abusive women finally left, I turned my mind to more practical matters. Knowing Tommy would be away for the best part of a week in the build-up to the Wembley final, I went upstairs to see if he had enough clean clothes for the journey. I opened his sock drawer next to the bed and gasped as I stared at a bunch of banknotes about as thick as a house brick. I'm ashamed to admit that I counted them but it was impossible to resist. There was exactly £4,000 in £10 notes. I didn't say a word about my discovery to Tommy upon his return. We were hardly speaking anyway.

It was against this background that Tommy prepared to lead out Manchester United against Liverpool in the 1977 FA Cup final on 21 May. A fixture like that should have been the last word in football romance. Maybe it was for others, but not for me.

THE LONG GOODBYE

O what a tangled web we weave,
When first we practise to deceive!
SIR WALTER SCOTT (1771–1832)

Tommy had left for London the previous Sunday without so much as a wave. United, ultimately a distant sixth to the champions Liverpool, had the unwanted distraction of having to play the final league match of their season at relegation-threatened West Ham United on the Monday night. We lost 4–2 and nobody apart from the reprieved Hammers remotely cared.

One of the unwritten rules that evolved in our partnership down the years was that, with the obvious exception of family emergencies, I wouldn't phone him in case I interrupted training, team meetings or media interviews. Instead, he would ring me. Before his departure, I asked what was troubling him. But he would just shrug and say, 'I'm fine.' It was all so out of character. The laughter had gone. I remember washing up after dinner one evening, staring out at the swimming pool and thinking, 'I don't laugh any more.' Life with Tommy had always been one long laugh. That, almost as much as anything else, worried me. I tried so hard to ignore the fact that I had seen similar signs before. The days of that week slowly passed without a single phone call from TD, so I broke our agreement and rang the Royal Lancaster Hotel on several occasions only to be told that he was busy.

The families and assorted club officials left for the game on Friday lunchtime to stay at the Royal Garden Hotel. My great friend, Doreen Blunstone, and I sat together on the train and, as the Cheshire countryside flashed past the window, my mind wandered back to the last time we were on our way to Wembley. I found it hard to believe that only a year had passed since we were surprisingly beaten by Southampton. Doreen had been very upset at the final whistle that afternoon and at one point on the long journey home she turned to me and said, 'When we come back next year, Agnes, we'll stay in the hotel and watch it on television. Agreed?'

In the aftermath of a Cup Final defeat, the last refuge of football folk is to defiantly say that you'll be back next season. Your heart yearns for it to be true, but your head and harsh statistics tell you that it very rarely happens. Yet there we were, 12 months down the railway track and back in the showpiece game of the season. Only this time, we were the underdogs to a Liverpool side chasing an unprecedented treble of League, Cup and European Cup.

I hadn't mentioned to a solitary soul that things were extremely difficult, although Doreen was also aware of

Tommy's strange behaviour. I know that now but I didn't know it then. It was only in the public fallout from the Mrs Brown affair that Doreen came to me and explained that, 10 years earlier, she had known all about the German woman. Many weeks after that train journey, and without any need, she apologised and spoke of the hours of soul-searching that she had endured back in 1967, before deciding not to tell me. I could never blame her. I would have hated to be in such an unenviable position. Doreen simply couldn't win.

I was still privately praying that whatever was troubling Tommy would resolve itself. He was clearly an unhappy man but I knew that it was in his own hands to remedy the situation. I had done all I could through unrequited love, patience and gentle persuasion to locate and then cure his problem without any comeback.

Catherine was almost four months pregnant and, on arrival at the hotel, declared she was starving and so we went off with her husband Dennis to the dining room. The restaurant was full, so we were asked to wait for a table in the bar. As we waited, who should walk in but Mrs Brown with her sister-in-law. I invited them to join us. At first she refused, but I insisted and she gave in and came and chatted with us for several minutes. As we eventually sat down to eat, I was aware of the frequent public address announcements for various wives of the United party to please go to the phone in the foyer. I was only too well aware they were receiving calls from loving husbands at the team hotel. Husbands who still had the consideration to think of their wives on the brink of such a defining moment in their careers. I listened with mounting frustration, aching to simply hear my own name being called out but it never came.

Early the next morning and after a fitful sleep, I bought a couple of newspapers in the lobby before taking a leisurely stroll through Kensington Gardens. Neither breakfast nor company held any attraction for me, so I sat on a park bench in the lukewarm sunshine and read the comprehensive Cup Final build-up, stopping to stare at the pictures of my smiling husband and remembering that was how he used to look when he was at home. When I eventually returned to the hotel, the official party was just beginning to board the two coaches for an early lunch at Wembley. I suppose it's quite strange in retrospect but, apart from my youngest and very excited son, Peter, the only other person I vividly remember watching climb on to one of those buses was an immaculately dressed Mrs Brown. In fact, on our way to Euston Station for the journey home, Doreen and I remarked on the many different, beautiful outfits the physiotherapist's wife had worn over the weekend.

I stood and waved them all off before returning to the hotel suite to order a selection of sandwiches and settle down with Doreen to watch the game on television. My emotions were very mixed but I was certain of two things. I wanted Tommy to win that trophy so very badly – and that, as a player and then manager, it was going to be fourth time lucky. I was so convinced that I also asked room service to deliver a bottle of chilled champagne in time for the final whistle.

Then came the five minutes of madness. We shrieked and danced around the room when Stuart Pearson put United ahead after 50 minutes but hardly had time to compose ourselves before Liverpool had equalised through Jimmy Case. Total elation to instant deflation. Less than three minutes later, a fluke goal for United. A Lou Macari shot that was drifting harmlessly wide deflected off the chest of Jimmy Greenhoff and slowly looped over the despairing reach of their goalkeeper, Ray Clemence. The remaining 35 minutes of the game were torture, but at last the final whistle blew. We'd done it! I was sure that whatever had been troubling Tommy would be banished by this long-awaited and deserved success. His celebrations on the pitch as I smiled through my tears at the television screen convinced me that my husband, balancing the lid of the trophy on his head during their lap of honour, would return and replace the stranger that he had become to me.

Time continued to crawl until the children eventually arrived back at the hotel in a state of complete euphoria, especially Peter. It was his first Cup Final as a spectator and we had won. He was almost delirious! Suddenly, everything was perfect as we commandeered the reception area and awaited the return of our conquering heroes. I may be a slightly-built woman but, when we saw the team coach pulling on to the forecourt half an hour later, I barged past anybody blocking my path, utterly determined to be the first to reach my husband. As I hugged, kissed and congratulated him, my love and delight for him were undiluted. I whispered into his ear, 'I'm so happy for you, darling, so very proud of you!' And it felt as though I had wrapped my arms around an enormous block of *ice*. It took my breath away.

On the way to a conference room the hotel had set aside for the occasion, he shoved a magnum of champagne and a pennant into my hands and ordered me to take them to the room. This was not *my* Tommy Docherty. On this of all days, he wanted me out of the way. Out of his life. I stared at him from a distance in disbelief until he came up to me several minutes later and in a voice so cold that again it made me shiver, he hissed, 'I thought I told you to take those things upstairs!' Instead, I went and placed them behind reception and returned to find him posing for photographs with another clutch of complete strangers. I practically had to beg him to have a family picture taken with the Cup.

TD seemed to avoid me every time I tried to make the slightest contact. I had been so looking forward to celebrating on our own, however briefly, to quietly savour the occasion. In my own way, I had worked just as hard for this moment as he had but I felt like an innocent bystander. Just another face in the crowd.

When the media throng and most of the hangers-on finally departed and everything quietened down, Tommy continued to find other people to talk to. I recall seeing Mrs Brown, again in an elegant gown, by his side and thinking she must be waiting for her husband, Laurie, to join them. I went over and stood by Tommy but continued to be totally ignored. I felt so embarrassed. At one point I did manage to murmur, 'What do you think you are playing at, Tommy?' but that too was brushed aside.

So, I collected the souvenirs from behind the front desk, took the lift to the top floor, showered and then dressed for the celebration dinner and dance. I was ready by the time he came to the room and automatically began to run a bath for him. As the taps spluttered into life, I couldn't stand the oppressive silence any longer. 'Please, Tommy, I've had enough of this,' I said. 'Why can't you just tell me what's wrong? Is it something I've done?'

He didn't even look up at me as he started to untie his shoelaces. 'I've told you before – nothing's wrong,' he sighed. 'How many times do I have to keep telling you? I just want you to leave me alone!'

As we walked into dinner, Tommy looked at the table plan and insisted that our daughter should sit beside him in my place. She didn't want to. She was angry with him, conscious of my discomfort and flatly refused. He really would have made a scene if I hadn't stepped in and asked her to change seats with me and sit next to her dad. It was only in an official photograph that I later noticed the close proximity of Mrs Brown on the adjoining table to my emotionally distant husband. The dinner slowly progressed but I could scarcely eat anything and merely rearranged my food around each successive plate before they were removed.

When Tommy was called upon to speak, he was barely able to mumble a few coherent sentences. This from the great raconteur and master of the one-liner. There were raised eyebrows around the room, I noticed, but people would later attribute Tommy's flat performance to the emotion of the occasion. From being upset, I was now genuinely worried. After the meal, he flatly refused to dance with me and again surrounded himself with television people and relative strangers. Even in my humiliation, I tried to stay alongside him – as best I could in a celebratory crowd – until he suddenly turned to me in front of several people and virtually spat, 'I thought I told you to leave me alone! Why don't you just get lost?'

I rapidly passed from concern, through fright to outright anger, but, having decided that I was not going to be forced out on this night of all nights, I went to the Ladies' Room. As I entered, I recognised the young wife of one of the United players. She was the only other person in there – and she was sobbing her heart out in front of the mirror, trying unsuccessfully to reapply her mascara. I held her tightly in my arms and asked her what on earth was wrong. I thought that perhaps the wine and the celebrations had all been too much for her.

She told me that she suspected her husband was having an affair with a nightclub hostess back in Manchester. He was being awful to her and she asked if I thought it might be a good idea to speak to Tommy about it. My God, if only that poor girl had known. We talked for some time until I managed to calm her down. I never told anybody the name of that distressed girl and I never will.

When I finally rejoined the party, several people came up to say that Tommy had been looking for me. When I found him, he was by now alcohol-fuelled and in fine fettle, singing like an out-of-tune lark and laughing at his own jokes. Although I was exhausted, I had no intention of going upstairs until he did so. But it was almost 6:00 am and daylight was breaking when TD and a group of his new-found friends decided to take the FA Cup for an early-morning stroll through Hyde Park. I went up to our room and sat staring out of the window at my husband noisily serenading the silverware in the park.

When he somehow found his way back to our room, I told him I was going to early-morning Mass. When I returned about an hour later, I was hardly surprised to find Tommy fully clothed and flat out. I removed his shoes, covered him with a blanket and sat there in silence while he slept. I was trawling through some of the heavier Sunday newspapers when the phone sprang to life on the bedside table with Tommy's alarm call. I sat and let it ring. He didn't hear a single thing. I managed to eventually awaken Tommy with a struggle and get him into the bathroom. He was in a daze so I talked to him constantly, reminding him of the TV interview he was due to give that morning. He shrugged and started to run the shower without uttering a single word.

Feeling nauseous, I went downstairs with one of the papers and sat where I knew I would be able to see him when he came out of the lift. When he finally did emerge, he looked around the foyer, saw me and walked straight out of the hotel to a waiting courtesy car. This was nothing to do with being short-sighted – this was absolute rejection. Why was I taking such treatment? It's a perfectly valid question but, if you have ever been fortunate enough to love somebody as much as I loved that man, you will also know the answer.

The next time I saw him was on the return train journey to Manchester. I was sitting at a two-seater table with Doreen while the team and directors were celebrating raucously in the next carriage along. Directly across the corridor from us sat Mrs Brown and her sister-in-law. Then Tommy came through carrying the Cup. I smiled proudly and called out to him. Once again, he totally ignored me and chatted happily with the other wives, families and their friends further down the aisle before going back to the adjoining coach. Within a matter of minutes, I became aware that Mrs Brown was crying. I leaned over to ask if anything was wrong. She apologised and explained that the book she was reading was very sad. And, at that precise moment, and for no specific reason, I remembered Maria. A young German woman crying in the back seat of our car years before. Instantly, I dismissed my thoughts as a flight of fancy, smiled weakly and silently told myself not to be so stupid.

On arrival at Wilmslow Station, we boarded a coach and followed the open-topped team bus past countless thousands of United supporters who lined the route all the way to Manchester Town Hall. At the civic reception, I stood at the back of the room as Tommy delivered another lacklustre speech.

A few moments after he'd finished, I felt Catherine tugging violently on my sleeve. 'Mum,' she said, come quick! It's Dad!'

Just after finishing his speech, Tommy had slumped into a chair, telling his daughter to come and get me. When I arrived, he looked so ill I decided I needed to get him out of there straight away. As we helped him out to the car, I couldn't help but think that at last whatever crisis Tommy had been building up to was now out in the open. We'd soon have him back to his old, laughing, happy self. I almost smiled.

He was utterly drained and his complexion matched his grey suit, except his jacket was so soaked in perspiration that it was beginning to turn black underneath the armpits. This poor, dear man was back to being a little boy again. Except that his deception and double life had finally caught up with him. Of course, I didn't know that then – or indeed that the worst was still to come.

He didn't utter a word throughout the 45-minute journey home, just gripped my hand – very tightly considering his condition. I helped him to undress, put him straight to bed and said that I was calling the doctor. He made me promise not to do so and demanded two sleeping pills. I had never needed such a thing – although I soon would – but he told me that he had some in his toilet bag, prescribed by the club doctor at Old Trafford. I gave him two aspirin instead. He swallowed them, fell backwards and slept almost around the clock until Monday evening.

Tommy slept for 22 hours straight. I didn't sleep at all. I knew we were heading for something – something awful that I could do nothing about. I felt sick with both worry and fear. We had finally won that godforsaken trophy and, at the same time, our lives were falling apart. FA Cup? Let's just call it a poisoned chalice and leave it at that.

By the time Tommy woke, he was very, very subdued. I tried to get him to respond as I busied myself around him with the housework but he behaved as though I wasn't even in the house. Then he insisted on going into Old Trafford. Under normal circumstances, I would have headed for the soapbox but I realised that I was back to treading on eggshells. He returned within two hours and went straight back to bed. Maybe he had gone in to make a private phone call.

He was very quiet the following day and spent most of it catching up on the sports sections of the newspapers. On the Wednesday evening, we had his favourite dinner of fillet steak, salad and new potatoes and watched Liverpool beat Borussia Monchengladbach 3–1 in the European Cup Final on television. Tommy lay back on the settee with his arms around me, enjoying several glasses of wine and the match. We had stopped the Scousers winning the treble and I knew that TD was thinking of his car resting on a distant Portuguese dock when he said, 'It's a shame, isn't it!'

I smiled at the ceiling and said a silent prayer of gratitude. Thinking, hoping, that some semblance of normality could now slowly return to our lives.

My contentment lasted until just before 11:00 pm, when he told me that he was going out. When I asked where he replied, 'For a meal.' Apart from everything else, he'd been drinking. I tried to talk him out of going but to no avail. He left, and it was almost 48 hours before I saw him again. There was no phone call on the Thursday and I had no idea where he might be. Eventually, I rang Old Trafford but Kath said he hadn't been there all day. That was unusual in itself. He arrived home slightly after 5:00 pm the following day, accompanied by a journalist 'friend'. I automatically started preparing some refreshments but Tommy went straight upstairs. I left the reporter in the kitchen talking to my brother, John, who had called in for a brief visit. I followed Tommy up to our bedroom and closed the door behind me. He said he was in a hurry and only had time to pack a change of clothes as he was the guest speaker at a dinner that evening in Northampton. Then he mentioned that he needed a holiday. I immediately agreed and suggested we should have an extended one, perhaps as long as a month.

Tommy's reply was delivered in a vicious whisper: 'I said *I* need a holiday.'

I answered, 'OK, my love, if that's the way you want it, fine – providing you are prepared to rejoin the human race on your return.' I then asked Tommy to please tell me what was wrong, what was happening to us.

He said, 'I am going my own way. Do you hear? My own way, on my own!'

I thought, 'On my *own*?' but replied, 'You always have gone your own way, Tommy, haven't you? What the hell are you saying – or trying to say?'

He turned around, his face contorted with barely restrained rage, and shouted, 'GET YOURSELF A BOYFRIEND!'

I was numb with horror. I thought that he was actually going round the bend. After his outburst, he began angrily throwing shirts, socks and underwear into a suitcase as I sat in silent turmoil on the edge of our bed. As he left the room, he said, 'Bring those two suits down.'

I did so automatically (I don't like the sound of myself here) and Tommy shared a few polite words with my brother before leaving.

I was on a mental tightrope without a safety net and I genuinely cannot describe the hurt, humiliation and torture I was suffering. Within minutes, Peter had returned home with two unannounced friends for tea, so I tried to concentrate on a pan of 15 fish fingers, think about chips and block out my runaway brain as best I could.

As John climbed into his car to leave, he asked me, 'What's biting him, love?' I had no answer.

On the Sunday afternoon, Peter and I went to Altrincham FC to watch an international youth-team tournament in which

United beat Celtic 2–1 in the final. From our seats in the main stand, Peter spotted Tommy in the VIP enclosure. He knew not to disturb his father at work, so I told Peter that his father would see him at home later. After we had arrived home, Peter sat on the wall by the front gate for over two hours watching every car come round the blind bend until darkness fell. I had to go out and tell him it was time for bed.

I went to bed in the downstairs guestroom, unable to bear the thought of any more scenes or unwarranted insults. I heard Tommy arrive home shortly after 2:00 am and go straight up to our bedroom. I waited for the sound of his footsteps coming back down to find me, to sit and talk to me, to tell me that I had only been dreaming. Most of all, I desperately wanted my husband back. I missed my friend. I thought I could have forgiven him in time but he was treating our house like a cheap hotel and making me feel equally worthless. I heard him emerge five hours later but I didn't call out. What would be the point? He closed the front door quietly behind him – his first thoughtful action in such a long time.

Four days later, at just after 11:00 am on Tuesday, 7 June, Tommy came home unannounced to collect some more clothes and brusquely told me he was travelling to Glasgow for a week to visit his mother. I didn't believe that for a second. He didn't like going back to his native city for any longer than was absolutely necessary, let alone to spend an entire week with his mother. There didn't seem any point in asking Tommy where he had been until now. I was only waiting for him to tell me what was causing this constant heartache.

Just over a week later, on Thursday, 16 June, Tommy called

to say he was coming home on Saturday night and that he had 'something important' to tell me. I told him that I wasn't prepared to wait that long. That I wanted him home that night, or else I'd go looking for him.

CHAPTER 15

GOING PUBLIC

Time is
Too slow for those who wait,
Too swift for those who fear,
Too long for those who grieve,
Too short for those who rejoice;
But for those who love,
Time is eternity.

HENRY VAN DYKE (1852–1933)

I don't know how long I sat there in the complete stillness of that night, endlessly attempting and constantly failing to digest the unpalatable truth. Tommy had come home that night and told me all about his affair with Mrs Brown – and that he was leaving me. It's a grossly overused word, but I was devastated. Isolated, wounding sentences ('I love her, I have to go') came swirling back as uninvited echoes through my tortured mind. I was unable to visualise any kind of future that could ever contain contentment.

Finally, as my tangled thoughts became too tiring to try to unravel alone, I phoned my good friend and family doctor, Dorothy Carlile, safe in the knowledge that she would respect my confidence. She anxiously asked me if there was an emergency because of the lateness of the hour. I hadn't even thought to look at the time. Dorothy came straight over and it was only in the remaining hours before daylight broke that I began to fully realise the dreadful strain of the last 12 or more months.

Despite Dorothy's medical and practical advice before she left, any attempt to sleep seemed totally pointless. Besides, my overriding concern was that Peter's life should remain as structured as possible on that awful Friday morning. The repercussions of his father's actions would violently invade his young life soon enough and forever more. But for now I was determined that some sense of false normality should prevail. And, until the late afternoon and Tommy's dramatic telephone call, I thought I had succeeded.

I kissed our wee boy goodbye as he scurried off to school. I then set about attempting to do my customary household chores, stopping only when Catherine made her daily morning phone call from Birmingham. Her pregnancy report may have been the reason I decided not to tell her of my torment. She – and the whole country – would know soon enough.

Then, just as Peter was due home from school, the phone rang. It was Tommy. There were no pleasantries – it was far too late for that anyway. He simply told me that, despite everything he'd said last night, he now wanted to come home 'Permanently, love' were the words he used, before adding,

'I'm so sorry. I know I've made the biggest mistake of my life.'

I was astounded and unsure how to react until I finally asked the only question that sprang to mind: 'What about Mrs Brown?'

He paused before replying, 'I've changed my mind. I'll tell her it's over when I get back. She'll be as sick as a parrot but she'll just have to get on with it.'

Honestly. At such a defining moment in our lives, he reverted to football-speak. Perhaps he was waiting for me to tell him that I was 'over the moon' or even that, 'at the end of the day, the boy done well'. Instead, I insisted I needed time to think and that he should come home and discuss it further. However, I was to be denied that opportunity. On the Saturday morning, I answered the door, half-expecting it to be my errant husband. It was Laurie Brown and tears were running uncontrollably down his cheeks as he stood helplessly on the doorstep, holding the trusting but trembling hands of his two little girls.

My initial instinct was to close the door on this man who had apparently been aware of the affair, but something told me that I should hear him out. I led him into the sitting room before taking Jane and Helen, then aged seven and four respectively, into the kitchen. Having given them some lemonade and biscuits and fetched the colouring books and crayons which I kept for visits by our grandchildren, I went back in to see Laurie. He was still in obvious distress, so I gently told him to pull himself together, if only for the sake of his daughters.

As we awkwardly talked, he strenuously denied that he had known of the affair between TD and his wife. His anguish seemed almost as raw as my own and I found myself believing him. I also said that I was surprised he should come to my home and then, for the life of me, I could not think of anything else to say. I also remember perhaps selfishly thinking that I had more than enough of my own problems to contend with and, if that was the purpose of his visit, he would simply have to find some other more sympathetic shoulder.

Laurie punctured the cumbersome silence by telling me how Tommy had altered team matters at United so that any player with even the slightest injury was told to report to the physiotherapist for treatment on Sunday morning. Until then, they'd always been given Sunday off. As it was extremely unlikely that no one in the team had suffered some sort of niggle during a match, Laurie had no alternative other than to go to the ground at lunchtime the day after every game and wait four or five hours for any players to arrive.

This happened every Sunday for 10 months – and on Thursday if there was a midweek game. I quickly realised that Tommy would tell me every Sunday that he was going into the office to catch up on his paperwork. So now we knew.

Then Laurie informed me that my husband and his wife had sold their story to the *Sunday People* and that it was going to be on the front page of tomorrow's edition. I was too taken aback to ask how he happened to know this and replied, 'Tommy Docherty will rot in hell.' What can you say about a man who leaves you, sells such a seedy story to the newspapers and then begs to come back before it's even published? Sometimes there are no suitable words.

With almost perfect timing, the phone rang. It was Tommy,

with more news: 'I'm sorry. I didn't mean to mess you about but I've decided I'm going to live with Mary after all...'

Laurie, who had been close enough to hear this, snatched the receiver from my hand and yelled, 'YOU BASTARD!' down the line.

No sooner had Laurie slammed the phone down than it rang again. I assumed it would be Mr Walter Mitty of Manchester (a.k.a. my husband) but it was Martin Edwards, at that time the junior director of United and son of the then chairman, Louis. He came straight to the point. 'Agnes, it's not true, is it?' he asked. 'Please tell me it's not.'

I said yes, unfortunately it *was* true.

Martin replied, 'Oh no, he's not going to Derby County!'

I took a deep breath before adding that I was unaware of any approach from another club – only that my husband had left me. I carefully and silently replaced the receiver as Laurie Brown left with his two wee girls. I neither saw nor spoke to Martin Edwards or Laurie Brown again. Nor would I have ever wanted to.

I thought I knew what to expect from the press once the news broke, but I was totally unprepared for the level of intrusion it would bring. The *People* was determined to get its money's worth out of the story, so I gathered my flock together and manned the barricades.

I called my second son, Tom, and told him to come home. I told him not to panic and that I'd explain everything when he arrived. I then telephoned Catherine's house and spoke to her husband, Dennis, and asked him to bring his wife over, again without going into detail. I was unable to locate my eldest son, Michael, who was out with his family visiting friends in Burnley. Peter, of course, was living at home but thankfully he was very busy at his school's summer fete on that particular day.

Catherine, Dennis and Tom arrived at much the same time in the late afternoon. I knew that my dishevelled appearance and puffed eyes prevented me from delaying the revelation. So I sat them down in the front room and, looking alternately at my two dear children, with an occasional and courteous glance towards my now ex-son-in-law, whom I never liked anyway, I recounted as best I could the conversation I had shared with their father two nights earlier and his subsequent phone calls. When I had finished – and it must have taken less than a minute – the boys didn't say a single word. My daughter responded by telling me she had been suspicious of her father on Cup Final night and had been concerned about us for some time.

Apparently, the previous summer while I was languishing in Lausanne, her father had said to her, 'You know, things haven't been too good between your mother and I for a couple of years now.' He also told her there had been other women in his life without revealing any names but, after much soul-searching, Catherine had decided to keep the conversation secret as she had not wanted to see me hurt. When a receptionist that my daughter knew in a Birmingham hotel told her that Tommy occasionally stayed there with a 'lady friend', she again remained tight-lipped.

And it was only now, almost 11 years later, that she unburdened herself of her own memory of Munich. On their visit to Germany, when she had accompanied her father at my insistence, I discovered that Tommy had sent Catherine off to school with Maria's daughter. Of course, with Maria's husband working during the week that left the two of them conveniently alone. On the first night of that trip with her father, Catherine had walked past the open door of the guest room and had seen Tommy and Maria sitting on the bed, whispering and holding hands. That 12-year-old girl, as she was then, had known it wasn't right – she just didn't know what or how to tell me when she came home. Like my friend Doreen, I could never criticise Catherine for keeping that information from me. She should never have been placed in such an unpleasant position in the first place.

When Peter arrived home from the school fete in a state of great excitement, he was instantly puzzled to find us all there. I had promised to present an autographed Manchester United football as part of the raffle and the organisers were wondering where I was. Something told me that now wasn't the time to shatter Peter's lovely little world forever, so I sent him back with the ball to apologise on my behalf. Now it was only a case of when I would tell him. I had to do it sometime in the next 24 hours, before the Sunday papers came out.

Peter returned home shortly afterwards and sensed from the strained and solemn atmosphere that something was seriously wrong. I gently took his hand and asked him to sit down next to me and told him, 'Your dad has left home to live with Mrs Brown, Laurie's wife.'

My wee boy's beautiful but disbelieving blue-grey eyes started to slowly fill as he looked at each of us in turn, sadly searching for individual confirmation. And then he uttered just one short word, perhaps the only word that someone of his age could think of at that moment in his young life capable of encapsulating all of his emotions. Great authors could pen a thousand words and never come close to emulating him. On his way to the downstairs bathroom, and without looking back, he said, 'Yuck.'

We heard him turn on the shower but that was merely a diversion. When he finally came back out after almost an hour, his hair was dry but the same couldn't be said of his eyes. I wish my husband could have been there to witness those scenes. In my opinion, Tommy never gave a solitary thought to his bewildered young son, his pregnant daughter, his elderly mother – to any one of us who until that climactic weekend had borne the surname of Docherty with such pride.

At about 7:00 pm at my request, Tom rang the *Sunday People* sports desk in Manchester politely demanding that they send a copy of their following day's front-page story for me to read. It arrived within 45 minutes. I'm convinced that their co-operation centred on the misguided belief that their story would elicit an instant and unpaid outburst from the scorned woman. After all, why would the messenger boy just so happen to be the sports editor? He even had the temerity to bring a staff photographer with him.

My husband was quoted thus: 'We are in love. We've got something special going for us and we've decided we would like to spend our future together. We haven't rushed into this. There's been a lot of soul-searching.

'The bond has grown between us and we've decided to bring

our relationship out in the open rather than live a lie. Mary and I plan to set up home together and hope eventually to wed.

'I've told Agnes of our decision and Mary has told Laurie. I believe that what has happened between Mary and me will be understood and accepted. It happens, after all, to other people every day.'

I was astonished that Tommy had been far more forthcoming to a national newspaper than he had ever managed to be to his own wife and children. Quietly and individually we read this proclamation of love – and digested it with similar degrees of disgust. It was almost 28 years since I had nervously waited for my fiancé and our future to come knocking at the door, telling me that I was going to live in England. Now, with millions of readers as witnesses, he was effectively telling me and our family to go to hell.

Tom was in charge of both the front door and the telephone and did a very diplomatic job. How fortunate for me to have a journalist son. I decided that I must ring a few close friends and relations to prepare them for what would be labelled an 'exclusive' the following morning. Tommy's younger sister, Margaret, almost made me laugh when I told her the news. 'My God,' she said, 'what kind of books has he been reading?' I asked her to make sure that Mrs Docherty knew before seeing the papers. I phoned my younger sister, Margaret, and my dear cousin, Agnes MacNeill, in Girvan. Poor Agnes. If you recall, she was the bridesmaid at our wedding and was so upset that I ended up comforting her. As I continued to make my calls, the children slowly and quietly retired to their rooms for the night.

My main concern had been for Peter. Fortunately, when I

had contacted everybody I considered important, I went upstairs and found him fast asleep. I stood in the shadow of his bedroom doorway looking at him for a long time, praying that he would overcome this terrible intrusion into his previously idyllic existence. I feared that such a dreadful experience would force him to grow up very quickly and could only hope that it would somehow make him a better man. Certainly better than his original role model.

Then I locked myself in my – no longer *our* – bedroom in the ridiculous hope of getting some sleep. From somewhere far outside of myself, I could hear enormous, racking sobs. It took me a moment to realise they were coming from deep within me. My whole body shook as I cried my heart out. I don't know how much later it was, but through my pain I somehow heard a persistent knocking at my door. It was Catherine, who had heard my distress and who wanted to make sure I was all right. I still automatically recoil from the vicious memory of that night.

As I slowly tried to recover, my trembling lips mumbled a promise to my pillow that I would never again cry for Tommy Docherty. It was a promise that I was unable to keep. I had no idea just how much heartache still lay ahead.

CHAPTER 16

TRIAL BY MEDIA

There is so much good in the worst of us,
And so much bad in the best of us,
That it hardly becomes any of us
To talk about the rest of us.

ANONYMOUS (C. 1897)

Tommy liked to have the national newspapers delivered. Every single one of them, every single day. Even the *Financial Times*. And yet he would only ever concentrate on the football pages. Even cricket, golf and rugby held no interest for him, never mind politics or reviews. But he would read the match reports, study the tables and digest the following week's fixtures until I was sure he must have memorised them. He would have put the most enthusiastic trainspotter to shame, but that was the nature of the man. He had travelled from 1940s Glaswegian to 1950s Lancastrian to 1960s Crombie. Now he was 1970s Anorak.

But on this morning I only had eyes for one newspaper, the

Sunday People. What I'd seen the night before had only been a photocopy. A part of me hoped it had changed since then. I was wrong.

THE DOC RUNS OFF WITH TEAM WIFE, screamed the headline. The dateline told me it was 19 June 1977. It was real after all. I was aware that at that moment people who were strangers to me all over the country were reading the same headline. Catherine couldn't understand my resigned attitude. 'Why didn't you just clobber him?' she asked me.

Although I had slapped him across the face twice at the height of his German affair a decade earlier, it had never entered my mind this time around. I loved him so much that all I had wanted to do was shield him from the eye of a self-imposed storm.

At first I failed to hear the sound of scratching but, inevitably, the news hounds were gathering at the door. I managed to slip quietly past them to attend early Mass, but by the time I returned an hour later the house was under siege. It was ridiculous. Surely there were more important events taking place in the world?

I literally had to force my way back into the house to discover that some bizarre auction had been taking place in my brief absence. My children informed me that hastily scrawled promises of huge amounts of money in return for my exclusive story had been landing on the doormat at regular intervals. One tabloid had actually increased its unanswered offer four times in less than an hour. I ignored them all. I still had my dignity.

The children were a tremendous source of strength to me

and it was they who decided that we couldn't stay imprisoned all day. With my neighbour Diana Davies's help, we escaped through our garden fence and into her house, from where we were able to slip out unnoticed. As Catherine was too pregnant to go over the fence, we decided to go through it. So there I was, in the midst of the emotional crisis of my life, wielding a claw hammer and giggling like an excited little schoolgirl as we carefully squeezed our way to temporary solace.

We eventually found refuge in a quiet country pub, where we ordered food that none of us ate. Peter excused himself and when he hadn't returned for some time I went in search of him. I found him sitting on a bench in the ornamental gardens in a very distressed state. Without the words to comfort him or indeed myself, I just silently held him. If Tommy could have seen his youngest son at that moment, then I wonder if... no, I'm being naïve. Remorse was no more a part of his make-up than humility.

When we returned home that evening, the reporters were still there. If anything, as we drove past the front of the house to then clamber back through the garden, they appeared to be increasing in number. Leaving the gap in the fence exposed for however long the siege might continue, we sat down in the lounge and turned on the television to watch the national news. Apparently, we had spent the entire day behind drawn curtains, refusing to answer the door or telephone. Through my suppressed tears, I nearly smiled.

I was determined that Peter should go to school as normal on the Monday morning, my one concession to the circumstances being that he should leave the house via the garden fence. I dreaded the thought of my innocent wee boy being interrogated by cynical reporters. As he set off, I rang his headmaster. He kindly offered to delegate a senior pupil to keep a protective eye on my son. Not always successfully as it transpired. In the ensuing weeks, my blameless boy suffered at school as the continuing publicity made him the constant butt of playground jokes. He didn't tell me. He didn't have to. Three times he came home with facial cuts and bruises and, on all three occasions, he claimed that they were the result of playing rugby. But a mother knows her children. Imagine a boy of that age feeling forced to defend the family name. And for what? It wasn't Peter who had besmirched it forever. As those dreadful days unfolded, his concern for me seemed to partially stifle his own distress.

By lunchtime, the number of circling media vultures had adopted a new tactic, abandoning my front door and hassling me by phone instead. After fielding call after call, Tom eventually suggested that I talk to the press. 'Just to let them see you, Mum. To let them know you are a *person*, not the "little wronged woman" they are all making you out to be.'

I told Tom that you cannot spread nearly 30 years of your life across the pages of a newspaper and do justice to the cherished memory.

Flowers, cards and letters were arriving all the time. It was heart-warming. I genuinely never realised so many people could care. It seemed to me that everybody was concerned, apart from the one person who had caused it all in the first place.

As the interminable days passed into even longer nights, I

found myself wondering where Tommy was, what he was thinking, what he was doing. Even if he was eating properly, for heaven's sake, but never, ever, who he was with. How do you disconnect yourself from being a loving and loyal wife? Are you meant to remove some sort of emotional plug from the socket on the wall before you go to bed every night? I would longingly listen out in the sleepless dark for the sound of him pulling into the driveway, of the car door closing and the front door opening. Most of all I missed the shared, effortless laughter that had been so special between us.

He will never be able to even begin or probably care to imagine the hell that he put me through. I loved him so very much. I know I've said it before but we were soulmates. I have frequently wondered if I would have submerged without my faith during those injurious days and yet, conversely, I found myself unable to pray. I could not relay my thoughts and feelings to anyone else – my family or closest friends – and so, when I was alone, I resorted to talking only to myself or the Almighty.

Matt and Jean were among the many people who kindly called round but, as with other guests, I could sense their discomfort and understood it. What could they do? I had been told that everybody at Old Trafford was aware of the affair and, therefore, in time-honoured tradition, I had been the last to know. But I could also tell that the Busbys had been kept in the dark because Jean was shocked and Matt was downright furious. He was always such a placid man, perhaps life had made him that way, but he naturally continued to carry great influence at United and was seething to the point where, although he didn't say it in so many words, I knew my warning to my husband about losing his job had been sadly correct.

Naturally, the media coverage of Tommy and Mrs Brown's affair continued unabated and with it my humiliation. I was watching my life being played out for public consumption. Try to picture what that's like. By now, it was Thursday, 23 June, and all the children were urging me to speak to a newspaper – if only as a means of attaining some peace. At that time, the amount of money involved (£30,000) wasn't an issue. I was absolutely convinced that Tommy would look after Peter and myself financially. However, I finally succumbed to the differing pressures and allowed two *Sunday Mirror* reporters and their photographer into my home that afternoon. I can't remember too much about the entire episode, except for strolling into the lounge, in as blasé a way as I could manage, to greet them with the remark: 'Hell hath no fury etc – isn't that what I am supposed to say?'

Catherine told me later that she was frequently forced to leave the room during the three or so hours of the interview. She found it too distressing to observe. Genuine roars of laughter at the memory of some shared moment with Tommy were apparently swiftly followed by me curling up into the chair and sobbing uncontrollably. I had always taken great pride in my privacy and now here I was, weeping in front of three complete strangers in my own home.

When one of the reporters returned the next day with a transcript of the interview for me to read and approve, I panicked. I told her I couldn't go ahead. It had never been my intention to waste anybody's time but I was instantly regretting my decision to play this particular game. Eventually my newly acquired solicitor, of whom much more later, issued an injunction to prevent the newspaper publishing whatever it was that I had said. Instead of making some money, I ended up with a large legal bill to pay!

I soon insisted that Catherine and Dennis should return home to Birmingham. Tom had stressed that he was moving back in for however long I needed him to be there and I was so grateful. Doctor Dorothy prescribed tranquillisers for a month or so, maintaining that they would help me to sleep. I was in no mood to argue. Perhaps it was the effect of the pills but I then went through a most peculiar phase. When I described the symptoms to a nursing friend, she nodded and told me not to worry, that it was commonly known as 'back to the womb syndrome'.

Without the assistance of an alarm clock, I would get up at 6:30 am precisely every morning and prepare breakfast for my two boys. When they had left, I would carry out the absolute minimum of domestic chores, fill a hot water bottle and go back to bed. I didn't answer the door, the telephone or any of my own numerous questions to myself. I actually slept. Somebody once called it the sleep of the righteous and my friend was absolutely correct. I would always wake up in the foetal position, clutching a by-now cold water bottle to my stomach and crying as uncontrollably as I must have done on the day I was born.

Sometime in the mid-afternoon, I would get up again in time for my sons returning home. It quickly became a vicious circle. I was unable to sleep at night and so I worked like a woman possessed. I suppose that's exactly what I was. Every wardrobe, cupboard and drawer was systematically emptied, cleaned and refilled. The windows were so clear they appeared to have no glass. As Tom and Peter slept, I knew it would be too noisy to hoover the entire house so I could be found ironing, cleaning the silver or reading – or trying to read. I just couldn't concentrate.

I was advised by Dr Joe Jacovelli, a colleague in the same practice as my friend, Dorothy, to see a solicitor. Initially, I hesitated but Joe insisted that it was important to safeguard my financial position and, without my agreement, sent a legal acquaintance of his to my house. Tommy later told me he was very surprised at this move, as I should have known the very least he could do was to look after Peter and I financially. I learned this with a wry smile and slow shake of my head through a letter from *his* solicitor.

I also quickly realised that, as soon as lawyers become involved between two people, the situation alters dramatically. Suddenly, almost daily and therefore expensive legal correspondence was discussing 'access visits' to our youngest son. Such laughable nonsense. Tommy could see Peter any time, anywhere, as far as I was concerned. However, it was arranged that he would come to the house at 11:00 am on Sunday, 3 July to see the boy he had walked out on in the night just two and a half weeks earlier.

On the morning of his father's access visit, Peter was nervous and sullen. I told him at breakfast that his dad would always love him, always be his friend. I also sensed he didn't believe a word of it and perhaps the passage of time has justified his original suspicion. When Tommy knocked on the door, Peter positioned himself at the furthest point in the lounge from where a kiss, hug or even a grown-up handshake would be possible. Our youngest son was polite but aloof. I hovered and eavesdropped as they awkwardly chatted about nothing, their conversation punctuated by long, embarrassing silences. They were virtual strangers because the man had never made the slightest effort to know the boy.

Then Peter called me and asked if he could be excused to go and play golf with a friend. I couldn't help but notice they had spent a total of seven minutes in one another's uncomfortable company and I'm not sure if they have ever spent longer together since that day. Tommy neglected to ever build a relationship with Peter. I saw this as another indication of his selfishness and the possibly misguided influence of other people.

As soon as Peter left, Tommy and I spent a surreal couple of hours talking about Manchester United. He asked for tea and a bacon sandwich – which for some unfathomable reason I made him – and talked incessantly about life at Old Trafford. Unprompted, he discussed the directors, players, staff and the coming season with himself at the helm. He was behaving as though life was normal and even went into the kitchen at one point to look at the fixtures on the calendars. I told him that there was no point – I had removed the calendar with the fixtures, plus I was also convinced he would lose his job.

Every Sunday newspaper in the land was debating whether or not a man's private life should interfere with his career. I considered the verdict a foregone conclusion. I knew I was biased, but I also remembered Matt Busby's reaction when he came to offer me his support. Tommy shrugged and nonchalantly smiled but I had studied the terms and conditions of his contract closely during one of my many recent sleepless nights and my tired eyes were constantly drawn to a particular paragraph that contained a clause relating to his future conduct as the manager of the club. It happened to allude to disrepute and dismissal in the same sentence. I didn't mention it to him that lunchtime but, without deriving any pleasure at all from the prospect, I was sorely tempted. I knew that it made the outcome a formality.

Tommy was sacked as the manager of Manchester United the next morning, 4 July. The statement, read by Les Olive, said, 'A meeting of the directors has decided unanimously that Mr Docherty is in breach of the terms of his contract and his engagement is terminated forthwith.'

I have always believed that the club showed a great sense of what could now be termed old-fashioned values in dismissing him. It must have been difficult for them as Tommy appeared to be on course for a period of sustained success and there may well have been those, including Martin Edwards, who were reluctant to let him go.

But the club did the right thing. Managers should lead by example. They have an unspoken responsibility to the many people who hold them in such high regard. Their principles and standards should be above reproach. Tommy had been irresponsible and deceitful to such a degree that how could he possibly manage and relate to young, impressionable players and ask of them qualities which he so very clearly lacked? I know, as a mother, that, if I had a schoolboy son with potential as a footballer, I would not want him being advised and influenced by such a man.

However, I must add that the loss of Tommy Docherty to football at the highest level of the game was very sad. He lived for the game, was a brilliant manager and so totally in love with United that everything and everyone else was of secondary importance. For such a career to spiral out of control was the greatest shame but he was his own worst enemy. He had so much left to offer but he was too easily led and ultimately that was the cause of his downfall.

And never more than in the immediate aftermath of his dismissal was this man of two halves so much in evidence. He will undoubtedly deny this to Mrs Brown and swear to her and anybody else prepared to listen that large swathes of this book are untrue. But why should I lie? What do I possibly have to gain? I didn't set out to write this book as a form of retribution. I just want people to know the truth.

The following Sunday, 10 July, the *People* published a story under the title: MARY BROWN'S OWN EXCLUSIVE STORY. In it, she said, 'I have been branded a wicked woman who has deserted her husband and children. That's not true. I haven't neglected my home and children. Until three days ago, I lived under the same roof as them. I haven't deserted them. I never would.' Don't worry, I've read that quote countless times and it doesn't make any sense to me either. 'Now all Tom and I want is to be left alone,' she added. 'I am very much in love with him and I believe he is with me.'

On the same day, the *News of the World* ran an exclusive

that I thought could be construed as unique in that paper's history. It had more than an element of truth to it. The headline said: 'A SECRET DOSSIER ON DOC', followed by the subtitle: 'Tycoon fans hired private detectives in 2-year probe.' I had heard on the football grapevine that some powerful people were intent on removing Tommy from office. I didn't know their motive, didn't ever mention it to my husband or anybody else for that matter. But I *did* have a reasonable idea as to their identity. They were always known as the 'Manchester Mafia' and, on the basis that I would like to sleep peacefully at night, even now I'm not prepared to divulge the name of a solitary member.

I didn't know all the details but the newspaper revealed that a team of detectives 'hired by a group of wealthy and influential businessmen' were told to spare no expense in building up the dossier that would lead to the manager's dismissal. Their investigations, it was claimed, centred around exactly how tickets allocated to United for the club's Cup Finals in the past two seasons had ended up in the hands of well-known touts; events surrounding Tommy's involvement in a car crash on his way back from the Sports Writers' Association's dinner in Glasgow; the allegations that he struck an 11-year-old boy outside a telephone kiosk and, of course, his affair with the wife of the club's physiotherapist.

A partner in the Stockport-based firm confirmed, 'We have carried out an investigation concerning Mr Docherty's conduct. But it would be unethical for me to tell you the nature of our enquiries or who was employing us.'

Late on Tuesday, 26 July, just over a fortnight after the

public account of their romance and commitment to one another, Mrs Brown's new love phoned me from a hotel in the Lake District and told me that he was staying there on his own for three or four nights. When I failed to respond to this unsolicited piece of information, Tommy then asked, 'Could we try and make a go of it again, please?'

I didn't hesitate for a second before telling him that it was far too late for that and hanging up. Just over an hour later, he rang back and, almost as if he hadn't remembered the first call, repeated the same question, word for word.

It was only when I'd put the phone down that his motive dawned on me. You would have to know Tommy as well as I did to even begin to believe his audacity. Perhaps he honestly thought that a media reconciliation, genuine or otherwise, might conceivably lead to his reinstatement at United. And that I would readily agree to it. Such was his state of mind, I thought, that he was even ignoring the fact that United had appointed Dave Sexton as their new manager 12 days earlier. He simply failed to recognise the full scale of the emotional destruction he had caused. I'm still not sure if he understands or not. But I certainly did. This was probably the moment when I realised that it was the end of Tommy and Agnes.

The following morning, Tommy's colleague Frank Blunstone asked if he could come round to collect the rest of Tommy's belongings. I found the task of sorting out his clothes and personal effects one of the most harrowing experiences of my life. The emotion caught me completely by surprise. In the midst of packing – yes, I actually folded everything neatly into all his suitcases – I suddenly had to stop and, slumping to the floor, recalled a similar exercise way back in the winter of 1954 when I had to clear out my mum's wardrobe after her death. That had been heartbreaking but this completely overwhelmed me. I sat and hugged his suits and shirts, smelling the faint traces of aftershave on the jacket lapels and feeling so rejected. It was actually worse than a bereavement. It would have been better to have lost Tommy in death because, quite simply, I could not have been more distraught.

After Frank left, I found myself tearfully removing our wedding photographs and snaps of other special occasions from their silver frames. It was equally traumatic but I knew it had to be done. Again, in death, family photos of the departed take on a whole new significance and become more precious than ever. Try to imagine how it feels when that person is still alive and living with another woman in the full glare of the national spotlight. If I'm being honest with myself, I didn't stop loving him during the weeks and months that followed. However, had I known what the next few years held in store, how much financial worry and public humiliation he would put me through, I think I would have hated the very mention of his name. The game was up; we were about to go into injury time.

CHAPTER 17

AND NOTHING BUT THE TRUTH

No poet ever interpreted nature
as freely as a lawyer interprets the truth.
JEAN GIRAUDOUX (1882–1944)

Peter Hardman was my solicitor. The alcohol killed him in the end but not before I lost any chance I had of securing the financial future of both myself and my youngest son. Certain people may wonder why, putting our fourth child to one side for a moment, I considered myself to be entitled to maintenance. Hopefully, as this particular chapter unfolds, they will understand.

Throughout our marriage, it was agreed that Tommy would look after the points and I would look after the pounds. I admit that he was spoiled but everything I did for him was a labour of love. Our income went on and into the home and, with four children, their partners, grandchildren and a relatively high standard of living and entertaining, the only money we managed to save was in the form of insurance policies and

Tommy's pension fund. We also had a company, Tommy Docherty Limited.

His earnings only ever started to look capable of keeping us in reasonably comfortable retirement from the day that Matt Busby picked up the phone. Apart from regular 'ghosted' newspaper columns and appearances as a television pundit, my husband had always been a born after-dinner speaker, with his natural wit and wealth of oft-exaggerated stories. His increased profile as the manager of Manchester United meant that, whenever he could spare the time, that aspect of his career started to soar. Tommy had no agent and often earned large sums in cash. He would derive great pleasure in returning from 'a free meal, free drinks and a great tip', as he once described it, and throwing £500 or more in used notes on to the kitchen table. How could I blame him?

Inflation permitting, Tommy was earning at just one of these speaking engagements more than he had earned in an entire year as a player at Preston North End. And he tried to be equally generous with the proceeds. I once rejected, with gratitude, the offer of a mink jacket and, on another occasion, he came back with a present of a heavy gold bracelet. I took one look at it and told him that I could never wear it as it would weigh me down. But I never lagged behind Tommy in pursuit of his ambitions. In fact, I ran all the way with him, from the beginning of November 1948. I was so thrilled to see him prosper.

Now I was staring at a thick file of solicitor's letters that, on a monthly basis, appeared to grow by the inch. Just a few examples of that correspondence will serve to illustrate how painful the marital breakdown process can be – and just how unforgivable Tommy's behaviour would ultimately become.

At the beginning of August 1977, TD was asked by his solicitor to complete a statement of his assets, income and outgoings. Unbelievably, he sent it to *me*, asking 'if I would mind filling it in' for him! I returned it immediately with the courteous suggestion that perhaps he should forward it to our company accountants, Alexander Simpson & Co. in East Molesey, Surrey.

The following week I received a note from him containing £160 in cash. 'This is just for food,' he wrote, adding, 'I hope it's enough – if not, please let me know. I'll try and do the right thing for you both as long as I live. I promise.'

Bitter experience has since taught me that such promises weren't worth the piece of paper they were scrawled upon.

It was legally established at an early stage that, including his bonuses of £15,000 from the previous season, Tommy had received £50,000 from United as compensation at the time of his dismissal. It was one of the few accurate figures he ever agreed upon in the entire protracted procedure. Perhaps he realised that I had so many friends in high places at Old Trafford that it would have been impossible even for him to dispute such a payment.

I realised one September morning, with a sinking sensation in my stomach, that, if he suspected for a moment that he could get away with anything, he would do or say whatever was necessary to achieve it. The bottom line? His word against mine.

Being married to such a person for so long had also taught

me that fame doesn't always turn only the head of its recipient. It can similarly cloud the judgement of an otherwise rational observer. I could only pray that, come the time, at least two of the local magistrates would be from the light-blue part of Manchester. I knew that if they were of the red persuasion then that could easily reflect the colour of my bank account for the rest of my life.

Within 10 days of my husband's postal delivery of money for groceries, I received correspondence from Mr Hardman informing me of TD's solicitor Mr Marco's proposal 'that £160 per four weeks be the level of interim maintenance for the two of you'. My lawyer went on to write: 'Mrs Brown has acknowledged receipt of the petition for judicial separation and indicates that she intends defending the case. I can only presume that she intends to deny the adultery alleged, and in respect of which your husband has made a verbal confession to you.'

This was just over a month after her *Sunday People* exclusive in which she was quoted as saying, 'It wasn't until last November that Tom and I realised how serious the situation had become. We started seeing one another about one night a week and on Sunday afternoons while Laurie was at the ground treating players injured the day before. We didn't book hotel rooms or borrow friends' flats or anything like that. If we had, the world would have known almost immediately.' She had neglected to mention that my husband had a key to her mother's flat, but I can only assume that people in such a position are somehow comfortable with such omissions, intentional or otherwise.

Mr Hardman's final paragraph concluded, 'I am told that

your husband is applying for unemployment benefit, a statement that is persuasive of the fact that he has no income. If this be the case, the recent payment of £160 must have been made out of his capital but we do not know the extent of his capital apart of course from his interest in the company. We still have no details of your husband's financial position and the manner of his support of you at the present is, to say the least, curious. The uncertainty is worrying.'

On 20 September, Mr Hardman wrote, 'I have now received a copy of your husband's acknowledgement of service of the divorce petition. He indicates that he does not intend defending the case nor does he object to paying the cost of the proceedings but he does reserve the right to make an application for custody of Peter and an application for access to see him. I think these statements are made more to protect your husband's position rather than indications that he will necessarily prosecute such steps, particularly an application for custody.'

During this avalanche of mail, a letter arrived for Peter. It was from his dad, telling our son how much he missed him and almost pleading with Peter to see him. My wee boy showed no desire to do so and, remembering their last awkward meeting in early July, I didn't want to force him or indeed hide anything from him. That was why I didn't mind him being in the room when I recounted a telephone conversation to my second son, Tom, that I'd had with their father the previous evening. At one point, Tommy said to me, 'It's been suggested to me that you must have been salting money away.' I didn't ask the source of such an insulting remark, stressing instead that everything was written down in black and white for his inspection at any time. He apologised before asking, 'Do you really need such a big house now?' I told him I had a large circle of family and friends and, after relaying the story to my sons, I assured Peter that this was our home and this was where we would be staying.

I had already replied to Mr Hardman, indicating that I was very anxious to resign from Tommy Docherty Limited, as I certainly didn't want to be involved when the Inland Revenue inevitably came calling. Talking of the taxman, Tommy was appointed as the manager of Derby County on 1 October. We were informed that his basic annual salary would be £20,000, but if I thought that might help to solve the financial wrangling I was very much mistaken. And I discovered as much upon receipt of a copy of a letter from his solicitors.

On 21 November, I received a letter from them informing me that, as he had received a 'substantial' compensation payoff from Manchester United, Tommy's tax liabilities for that year were such that his lawyers and accountants were arranging for him to waive his Derby County salary until the beginning of the next fiscal year, 1978/79. The letter concluded, 'There is no question of our client taking any steps to avoid payment of income or of capital to your client. It is just a question of arranging his financial position in order to avoid the Revenue swallowing everything that he earns.'

And so it went on into the new year, the lawyers playing their schoolyard games of 'My dad's bigger than your dad'. On 27 January, Mr Hardman wrote to Mr Marco to explain, among various other points, that: 'Our client states that, shortly before the 1977 FA Cup Final, your client had £4,000 in cash at the matrimonial home. Our client is aware that your client took this money with him when he left the house. Can your client state what happened to this fund?'

Almost five weeks later, on 1 March, Mr Marco replied, 'Our client has no knowledge of the existence of this alleged sum of £4,000.'

So, I later told Mr Hardman, I must have had simply imagined finding 400 £10 notes bound together by two green elastic bands in a bedroom drawer. I may have had a hellish year but I certainly wasn't hallucinating. The next paragraph in Mr Hardman's letter continued: 'Our client tells us that the building society account in the name of Tommy Docherty Limited of which, you may recall, our clients are the sole directors and our client is the secretary, has £2,144.00 invested in it and the company's bank account is in credit £77.09. In the past, the fees received by your client in respect of personal appearances, advertising, endorsements, revenues from books and fees for public speaking engagements have been credited to the company's account. In recent months, very few payments have been received from your client for the credit of the company's account, though it is understood by our client that your client's fee earning services have continued and, of late, have increased. Will you please ascertain from your client if he has received fees for fee earning engagements which have not, in fact, been credited to the company.'

The response to that enquiry simply staggered me. 'We are instructed,' wrote Mr Marco, 'that our client is not at present receiving any fees derived from work carried out outside his immediate employment as manager of Derby County Football

Club. He has been told by his accountants that because of the very high marginal rates of tax which will apply to income earned in this way, it is simply not worth his while charging any fees. Accordingly, any personal fees etc. made by our client are done so purely on a charitable basis, save that every so often he receives £10 or £15 for appearing on television or radio, but here again the amount of tax payable on these sums renders them virtually valueless.'

That begs a fairly obvious question. Why do it at all?

Part of a further letter from Mr Marco on 30 June said, 'We believe that one of the outstanding points raised in earlier correspondence by you with regard to any payments made to our client were the newspaper articles when he left Manchester United. We are able to confirm that he received no payments from any newspapers.'

On 16 August, I received something in the post regarding Tommy that I actually knew to be true. His solicitor sent me, via Mr Hardman, a photocopy of my husband's 'Confession of Adultery'. I was told I had to identify Tommy's signature for legal purposes. Dated 5 August, the statement, in an almost matter-of-fact manner, read as follows: 'I was married to Agnes Docherty on 27 December 1949. I last lived with my wife in June 1977. After I left my wife, I committed adultery with Mary Brown at Whitegate House, The Mudd, Mottram in Longdendale, Derbyshire. Adultery has occurred frequently since that occasion and I am living with Mary Brown.' Well, '*After* I left my wife' indeed.

Around this same time, I was also told to surrender my marriage certificate. No matter what you may feel about your former husband, there is an element of sentimental value about that piece of paper. On phoning the relevant court department at a later date to enquire as to its whereabouts, I was brusquely informed, 'Didn't anyone tell you? You don't get it back.' It was almost as soul-destroying to see my marriage now being 'put asunder' by post as it had already been in the newspapers. I use those words from the Bible because I clearly remember them from my marriage ceremony: 'What therefore God hath joined together, let not man put asunder.'

I was ordered to attend Manchester County Court at 10:30 am on Tuesday, 24 October, with regard to the custody of Peter, who had just turned 14. It was my first experience of being in court and I felt as though I was in some kind of horror movie. Tommy had neglected to build a relationship with any of our children except Michael – and even then football was the single common denominator – and I knew that my youngest son wanted to live with his father about as much as I did. Mr Hardman promised me that it was merely a formality. My representative presented Peter's academic and sporting abilities and the reasons why I should be granted custody. Although the three magistrates thankfully arrived at their predictable verdict after all of 12 minutes, I was shaken to the core by the proceedings.

At the end of the football season the following May, something happened that I would never have imagined possible. Having just survived the drop in Division One, Tommy resigned as the manager of Derby and went back to relegated Queens Park Rangers – and Jim Gregory.

On the same annual salary of £20,000, I could only assume they had both either forgotten or decided to overlook his disastrous 28-day reign 12 years earlier. TD was quoted thus: 'Obviously I am delighted to be joining the club and it is always nice to know that you are wanted. It was the chairman who enticed me back. He is a man of decision like myself and showed he wanted me.'

All I wanted was a resolution to the endless legal battle and, as the days dragged into weeks and months, the date for the financial settlement finally arrived: Thursday, 18 October 1979. Four days had been set aside for the case, but it was completed before the end of the first day. I attended with Mr Hardman, his clerk and a QC. Tommy had three similar representatives and his new accountant. I was in a very emotional state. I had hoped the awful experience of almost exactly a year earlier, when I 'won' custody of Peter, might have prepared me for this new trauma. It didn't.

It was far too late but I felt sure that if TD and I could have sat down quietly on our own somewhere then the situation would have been resolved satisfactorily. As it was, he eventually offered a settlement figure of £25,000 – the same amount, I reflected, that he had been paid for selling the exclusive story of his deception to the *Sunday People*. Mrs Brown had just given birth to their first daughter and the tabloids were having a field day yet again. Such perfect timing.

Towards the end of the adjournment for lunch, I sat in a corner with Catherine and we watched and whispered as the lawyers incessantly paced the corridors. One lot would offer a slightly increased figure and then the other lot – my lot – would approach me for my reaction. The choice of the word 'lot' is purely intentional. I felt as though my entire life – my wonderful past, my miserable present and my uncertain future – was being auctioned off.

Predictably, the press boys and photographers were hovering in the shadows. I was only insistent to Mr Hardman on one aspect of the case, and that was to refuse a settlement figure. I didn't want Tommy to walk away that day with no future commitment to Peter and I. Every single month, I was determined that he should be forced to remember what he had done – not just to pay the price financially. I wanted us to at least live on in his conscience because, on that dreadful day, I still believed that he actually possessed one.

Before, that is, I considered the offer of £25,000 for almost 30 years of my life. Less than £1,000 a year for everything that I had contributed to our marriage and his success. I regarded it as derisory and then, to add insult to injury, I was informed that the figure was not to include our house. That afternoon, maintenance was set at £9,000 per annum for me and £1,000 for Peter (£522.39 and £58.33 net per month respectively). The Elms was ordered to be 'sold forthwith', with the proceeds to be equally split and *I* had to keep paying the monthly mortgage of £233.83 and rates of £65.36 out of my allowance until the property was sold. I was also made liable for 'gas and electricity accounts and all other domestic expenditure'.

Just over one year earlier, in his Affidavit of Means at Manchester County Court, Tommy had stated, 'Pending a decision as to capital by this Honourable Court I would respectfully submit that I undertake to make the mortgage repayments on the former matrimonial home until it is sold.'

If only I could relive that day again. If only I could have managed to control my emotions enough to say what I really thought. If only...

We had no further contact until Tommy rang around noon on Tuesday, 4 December, to tell me that his mother had died the previous day. I sympathised with him and promised I would be at the funeral with our two younger sons the following morning. He was travelling up to Glasgow with Michael and, without my mentioning it, promised that Mrs Brown wouldn't be there and that he would also give me the cost of our flights in cash when he saw me. We were met by Ken Gallacher, a Scottish journalist friend, who drove us to the Requiem Mass and back to the airport four hours later.

As we walked away after the burial, I turned to see TD standing alone at the graveside. Thinking he might be in difficulty when he finally looked up (he suffers from vertigo), I went over, took his hand and led him away. Michael, Tom and Peter were waiting at the gates of the cemetery and their father, with tears in his eyes, glanced across at them and murmured, 'My sons...'

Three days later, Tommy was travelling home on the 19:25 pm London to Manchester inter-city express after QPR had drawn 2–2 at home to Wrexham. On the same train were several hundred Manchester City fans who had just seen their side lose 4–0 at Ipswich. Wrong place, wrong time. It seemed from various front-page Sunday-newspaper reports the next morning that Tommy had objected to 'supporters around the buffet bar singing an obscene song with particular reference to Mary Brown'.

The stories went on to allege that, just before alighting at Stockport station, Tommy had thrown the first punch and that, as a result, he had arrived on the platform slightly quicker than he had anticipated – underneath the considerable weight of several City supporters. When their flailing fists had finished, Tommy was transferred by ambulance to the local infirmary, suffering from multiple head wounds and ruptured leg muscles. I decided to wait for a couple of days before visiting him with a couple of bottles of what he always called Scottish champagne – Perrier water!

I didn't know that Mrs Brown would be there when I arrived but the ward sister, clearly aware of the delicate situation, asked me to wait in her office and went to enquire if he wanted to see me. Mrs Brown left his room and I went in and spent about 15 minutes with Tommy. What with the cemetery and now the hospital, I'd seen more of Tommy in the past 72 hours than I had in who knows how long. He appeared embarrassed, showed me his scars and thanked me very much for coming. We didn't really have anything much to say to one another – until I was just about to leave.

As I reached the door of his private room, he said to me, 'I was lucky, wasn't I?'

I glanced at his left leg, the same leg he had broken in 1953 when we were in Preston and the world was young. 'You certainly were!' I said.

'No,' he replied, looking down at the plaster. 'Not this. I meant in court.'

I had no reply to that, so I slowly walked out through the main hospital entrance and past the phalanx of waiting photographers. They didn't flash a bulb and it dawned on me that they had no clue as to my identity. I liked that. Until I drove home in tears – all the way home in tears. She who was never going to cry again!

CHAPTER 18

PROMISES, PROMISES

You'll want for nothing, Agnes.
TOMMY DOCHERTY

That unsolicited promise is one of the very few phrases that I can recall with any clarity from those hazy days. By April 1980, six months after the court order, the maintenance payments had become so sporadic that, on any given month, Tommy was paying all of it, some of it or frequently none of it, leaving me frightened to answer the front door.

Ask any rejected wife the first thing she notices after the man she worships walks out of that door. It's her self-esteem that goes first. You just feel so *unwanted*. I could barely get up in the morning some days. I even stopped brushing my hair. And yet, you eventually come back. With the greatest respect to other nationalities, I firmly believe there is a fundamental survival streak in Scottish people. I was *not* prepared to allow that man to destroy me, my family or the rest of my life.

However, due to electricity, gas and telephone bills and the general cost of even frugal living, I was almost £1,200 overdrawn at the bank, the mortgage and rates were due again and I was having to buy expensive chlorine tablets for the swimming pool. Define irony. Maintaining the pool while my husband clearly felt that he didn't have to maintain *us*.

At the beginning of May, and I can't say I was shocked, TD was sacked by Jim Gregory after QPR finished fifth in the Second Division, missing out on promotion by just four points. In the wake of protests from both players and supporters alike, the chairman reinstated him nine days later. 'He has been a magnificent chairman to me,' Tommy later told the press on his reprieve. 'We have never really had a cross word.'

There were plenty heading his way, though. Two weeks later, in a letter to his solicitor, Mr Hardman wrote, 'As is well known, pending completion of the sale of the matrimonial home, our client's income is substantially eroded by defraying the mortgage and the rates on the house. Having honoured her part of the agreement, our client finds it uncommonly hard that your client, without prior warning, should so reduce the maintenance payments as to leave her with little, if any, money for such necessaries as food and clothing. Will you please intercede as rapidly as possible to prevent the financial situation from deteriorating further and ensure that forthwith your client makes up the substantial shortfall which already exists. If it should be that all the arrears are not made up by your client within seven days, enforcement proceedings will be taken without further notice. It would, indeed, be a matter for regret if such steps had to be taken but your client's approach leaves us with no alternative.'

Unbelievably to me, that undisguised threat didn't even elicit a reply. However, instead of carrying out his warning, Mr Hardman told me that he was seeking to deduct the debt from Tommy's share of the eventual sale of the house, but it didn't happen that way. To compound my misery, the house market was equally depressed at the time and it wasn't until early July that the Elms was finally sold at the giveaway price of £87,000.

I received £45,000. By the time Tommy had repaid the outstanding mortgage of approximately £18,000, he pocketed £24,000 as his reward for leaving us for another woman and the maintenance arrears continued to accrue. Is there anybody out there who can explain the justice of that to me? I had thought when I no longer had the high mortgage and rates payments to meet that I would be better off but that didn't happen either.

I felt that I had to buy a new house outright as I didn't want the worry of a mortgage hanging over me and Peter. While I moved to a considerably smaller property two miles away at 7 Fountain Avenue, Hale, which cost £41,000, I learned that Tommy, Mrs Brown and their children had installed themselves in a beautiful cottage in the Derbyshire village of Charlesworth, near Glossop. In contrast, I had to clear an overdraft that was now nearly £2,000 and exchanged my BMW for a Talbot Sunbeam 1.3. It was then, in desperation, that I decided to circumvent the solicitors and write directly to Tommy, asking him to '*please* rectify the matter immediately'.

'The last four years,' I continued, 'have been very trying and heartbreaking so please fulfil your duty to Peter and myself. I know – or can only guess – the demands upon you but first things first my husband, OK? You are *lawfully* bound on this matter and my solicitor has talked of a summons but I sincerely don't want to cause you any trouble. I hope my plea will be heeded. I feel humiliated enough without having had to write this note. I await your immediate action on the matter.'

By return of post, I received a cheque from Tommy for £1,878.50 – the total amount of arrears. Then, at the beginning of October, Jim Gregory wielded the axe at QPR once and for all, causing my erratic maintenance to become consistent. Consistent in that it stopped altogether.

With little or no choice, I applied for a job selling women's clothes at the department store Rackhams in the nearby town of Altrincham. I remember once, when our daughter, Catherine, was aged about 15, she said to me, 'You haven't worked since you married, Mum, have you?'

I politely asked her to rephrase the question! I was very nervous about the interview but I was offered and accepted the post there and then. My salary was £1.45 an hour for a 22 ½-hour week and I enjoyed it very much. It was nice to be among people again – even if I was the subject of everyone's curiosity as 'the Doc's wife'. I had only mentioned it in friendly conversation with my supervisor but that's all it takes when perceived fame enters the frame.

I managed the first year on the shop floor without too much trouble but then, probably because I had doubled my weekly working hours through financial necessity, I would arrive home suffering from complete exhaustion and excruciating pain in my neck and shoulders. I also occasionally worked at night as a waitress for my friend, Ruth Gore, in the catering business, and babysat for three families.

Doctor Dorothy strongly advised me to pack in my day job as, by now, I had been diagnosed as suffering from spondylosis. Also known as spinal osteoarthritis, it's a degenerative condition of the cervical spine that is normally attributed to old age. In my case, it was the direct result of my leap in the larder and subsequent surgery. I desperately needed the money, insufficient though it was, but I also realised my long-term health and ability to look after Peter were far more important considerations, so I reluctantly handed in my notice with immediate effect.

On 6 November, Mr Hardman wrote, 'Mr Docherty is on the point of filing an application to lead to an Order reducing the amount of the existing maintenance orders for Peter and yourself because he does not have employment at the moment. If at the hearing date we are unable to show that he has, for example, substantial funds of capital on which to live, there is a distinct possibility that the Court will have no option but to reduce the amount of the orders.'

I sat for a long time that morning, dumbstruck at the audacity of a man who, according to various reports, received £10,000 compensation for his dismissal at QPR, continued to earn large sums in cash on the after-dinner circuit and was now seeking to lower the amount of maintenance that he wasn't even paying. Within weeks, Mr Hardman was back with more news: 'His solicitor has now informed me that Mr Docherty has a job for the next nine months as Coach to the Sydney Olympic Football Club in Australia, his remuneration for the period of the contract being £20,000 (Sterling) plus, of course, his travelling expenses. His solicitor is seeking confirmation that arrangements will be made by his client to continue making payments at the rate of the Orders whilst he is abroad.'

Tommy rang me in the middle of the night on several occasions from Australia, never stopping to consider the time difference and with precious little to say other than the repeated assertion that I would 'want for nothing'. I began to seriously consider the possibility that he misunderstood the phrase.

At the beginning of June 1981, Tommy was on his way back from Down Under to take over as manager of Preston North End, newly relegated to the old Third Division. It had taken him nearly 32 years to come almost full circle, but by December he had been sacked again.

He continued to keep in touch by telephone, sometimes as much as three times a week, then there would be fairly long periods when I didn't hear from him. He arrived on my doorstep that Christmas laden with gifts for Peter and me and then came to see me the following February on my 53rd birthday with presents and flowers.

On 20 March 1982, he sent me a beautiful bouquet for Mother's Day and then rang that afternoon to check I had received it. I thanked him before adding, as I was being pressured by the bank about my overdraft, that I would have preferred the money instead of the flowers.

'If you want to play it like that, okay,' he said and hung up.

By now, he was living with his new family in a converted coach house in Charlesworth and the nearby cottage, naturally in Mrs Brown's name, was up for sale at £74,000.

The years slowly changed on my single calendar but precious little else did. I would receive a cheque for £500 here and a drunken phone call there – the latter sadly far more frequently – until, on Friday, 23 January 1987, almost a decade after Tommy had deserted us, I was back at Manchester County Court seeking to obtain maintenance arrears of £9,450. And it wasn't even mine. It was money that I owed the bank.

Tommy's solicitor secured an adjournment on the basis that I hadn't signed the Final Decree papers. Quite honestly, it didn't matter to me one way or the other but I had been advised against doing so by Mr Hardman. I didn't understand the legal implications except that it now seemed my apparent refusal to grant my husband a divorce was infringing the maintenance agreement. The fact the arrears were so substantial was almost being treated as incidental. So, I went home, signed and immediately sent off the document. I was subsequently told I didn't have to attend court, that it was merely a formality. So it was that we were divorced on Thursday, 12 February, and I received a letter informing me that 'on the above date it was decreed that the marriage solemnised on 27 December 1949, between Thomas Henderson Docherty and Agnes Docherty is dissolved and the decree is final and absolute'. An early 58th-birthday present.

We were back in court on Monday, 23 March, for what would be the final time – and the last fixture that I would ever write down. Docherty v Docherty.

The arrears were now exactly £10,500, plus bank charges, and interest of £1,113 on my overdraft. A total of £11,613. The tabloid reporters were claiming that I wanted Tommy imprisoned if he didn't pay the arrears in full. Such nonsense. Mind you, he would probably have survived prison quite happily and made money from the experience. No, I couldn't wish a jail sentence upon him – not even when he sat opposite me that morning and announced himself bankrupt!

As Catherine and I sat in the cold corridors, watching the lawyers bustle back and forth, we noticed that Mrs Brown seemed to be doing all the talking – or perhaps that should be negotiating – while Tommy just sat there and occasionally shrugged his shoulders. Eventually, Mr Hardman joined us and said the final offer was £15,000 and that I 'should accept it because it's all you're going to get'.

The arrears and bank charges were included in this final payment, so I was effectively being written off for £3,387. Since TD was now bankrupt, I would never again receive any maintenance in my lifetime.

He had not only left me, he had also left me virtually destitute.

CHAPTER 19

MOVING ON

For when the One Great Scorer comes to
mark against your name,
He writes – not that you won or lost – but how
you played the Game.

GRANTLAND RICE (1880–1954)

The tabloids and television now refer to them as Footballers' Wives, but the likes of Elsie Finney, Jean Busby and I always preferred to call ourselves 'grass widows'.

And, in that respect, it would have been easier if Tommy had died rather than put me through such undeserved torment. In fact, I think that in the years that followed, and in spite of the all too frequent patches of publicity, I actually did come to treat our separation as a form of bereavement.

In the way that you mourn the passing of a loved one, it allowed me the space to grieve and then eventually to continue with my own life. As the seasons changed – and for the first time in my adult life, thank God, they were no longer of the football variety – I learned to enjoy my own company.

Heady stuff, this freedom. Often turning down invitations from my children or close friends for occasions such as Christmas Day dinner or birthday parties, I would apologise before genuinely delivering my stock phrase: 'I may be *alone* but I'm not *lonely*.' There is a massive difference and it's true – time does heal! It took me so long to come to terms with my situation, but I have succeeded.

I also think it's one of the few things that Tommy has never managed. Although I was finally able to move on, I don't believe that Tommy could remove me from his affection or assuage the remains of his conscience. I don't think he ever will. Please don't misconstrue that as arrogance on my part because you probably realise by now that I can provide dates as evidence. Days and times when, outside and even long after our maintenance battles in court, I continued to be the only person it seemed that he could turn to in times of inner turmoil.

For example, he called me on Saturday evening, 11 May 1991, and I instantly knew from the way he said, 'Hello, it's me' that he was drunk.

After he had slurred through his blurred mind for almost a minute, I decided it was time to interrupt him. 'Tommy,' I asked, 'what exactly *is* it that you want?'

He paused before answering, 'I've always loved you.'

I said 'Bye' and put the phone down.

Each year has brought calls, cards and occasionally what he would probably consider financial compensation. On Wednesday, 22 December 1999, I received a Christmas card that inside contained the printed words: '…and a happy new Millennium'. Below it, Tommy had written, 'Well, as best you can, TD x.'

Of course, the hurt never goes away entirely but one buries it so deeply that it isn't always possible to exhume it for examination. Except, that is, for the tiniest, niggling voices that refuse to rest in peace. All this time later, certain words or phrases continue to reverberate. For some reason, by far the most frequent visitors are: 'You gave me too much rope and I've hanged myself.'

The reason I equated that rope to trust was because, for almost 30 years of my life, I was the wife, best friend and champion of Tommy Docherty. I have never considered myself a failure in the fact that I was the victim of a broken marriage. Rather, I think my ex-husband was the one who failed. He could not appreciate and remain faithful to a relationship in which he was passionately cared for in every way. But I feel lucky. We had so many wonderfully happy years together and I genuinely thank him for every one of them. It is a good average by any standard, especially in today's world.

Strange to reflect, therefore, that Tommy didn't so much leave me as I finally let him go. It took a considerable amount of time for me to realise that I didn't make the same great effort to keep our marriage together that I had 10 years previously. Part of me suspects the reason was that I had four young children to support and care for back in 1967. A decade later, I just felt so incredibly weary. Subconsciously, I must have thought I couldn't rebuild those broken bridges or once again accept his false promises after all the pain he had inflicted.

Tommy put me through hell but, poor man, he was living in a hell of his own. I hope it has all been worthwhile for him and, as ever, I wish him well.

He has had to live with the consequences of his actions, as indeed I have. I wonder which of us was the better survivor in the years that were to follow. I know he hasn't been through the emotional agony and penny-pinching that I have had to endure, but perhaps I have somehow been paying the price for so many blissful family years. They were the important times when the career, the rapport, the closeness and the very existence of our healthy children and grandchildren made life so special.

I would go to sleep at night excited at the prospect of waking up alongside him the following morning. We were young together and so very much in love. He may not admit it – except in quiet moments to himself or if he can ever summon up the courage to stare into that unforgiving mirror and remember – but I continue to believe that there is a part of TD's heart which will always love me.

When I consider the trail of emotional destruction that man left in his wake, I find it so ironic to look back on the first few months of 1953, when I lost a son as a mother and he lost the championship as a player. I can see now that there was a tragically perfect symmetry. Family was all that ever mattered to me but, for Tommy, it was always football.

I know the enduring success that Sir Alex Ferguson has enjoyed at Old Trafford gnaws away at the very core of Tommy's being. He has never told me that but he doesn't need to. The trophies and subsequently stratospheric salary, the adulation, the knighthood. Because I know, he knows, that they were his for the taking. There's really only one direction to go after being sacked as the manager of Manchester United but I feel far more frustration than satisfaction that Tommy's career went rapidly downhill from the moment he left me.

I did ask myself the question on so many sleepless nights: where did I go wrong? Hand on heart, I could never answer it. I read somewhere that it takes two to make a marriage but only one to break it. I have to disagree on the basis that it took two to break my own. How can they have ever trusted one another in the ensuing years? When you have witnessed at first hand how callously a person can lie and cheat their way through any situation, how can you possibly rest assured that one day they won't do the same to you? The simple answer is that you can't. I don't consider that to be much of a basis for a loving relationship.

And yet it really doesn't matter any more. My life has almost run its course and, without the slightest feeling of bitterness, I can genuinely say that his second wife is more than welcome to the man he is today.

Because I knew Tommy Docherty when he was worth knowing...